The Vegetarian Gourmet

THE
VEGETARIAN GOURMET

315 International Recipes
for Health, Palate, and a Long Happy Life

SALLY and LUCIAN BERG

HERDER AND HERDER

1971
HERDER AND HERDER NEW YORK
232 Madison Avenue, New York 10016

Original edition: *New Food for All Palates: A Vegetarian Cook Book.* © 1967 by Sally and Lucian Berg, published by Victor Gollancz, Ltd., London.

Contents

Acknowledgments

We wish to make particular acknowledgment to Dr. B. M. Lal of Hyderabad City for his generous and invaluable help with our Indian section.

We also wish to thank that unique man and surgeon, Dr. S. Galewski, for the information on Chinese rickshaw men and the Kempner Diet.

Thanks, too, are owing to our friend Krish Patel for showing us the story *The Miraculous Monkey*, and Senhor Jorge Branco for contributing Portuguese recipes.

The following acknowledgments are for permission to quote extracts from copyright material:

Allen & Unwin Ltd.: *Man in Search of his Ancestors*, 1955, by André Senet, translated from the French by Malcolm Barnes.

A. & C. Black Ltd.: *The Schweitzer Album*, 1965, compiled by Erica Anderson.

Columbia University Press, New York: *Early Chinese Literature*, 1962, by Burton Watson (translation of Ode 279, *Shih ching*); *The Poetry of History*, 1947, by Emery Neff (translation of extract from Herder).

Michael Joseph Ltd.: *Promise at Dawn*, 1962, by Romain Gary; *The Chinese Gold Murders*, 1959, by Robert van Gulik.

Mr. Walt Kelly—creator of *Pogo Possum*.

Oxford University Press: *Three Japanese Plays*, 1959, edited with introductions by Earle Ernst (translation from *The House of Sugawara*).

Penguin Books Ltd.: *The Penguin Book of Japanese Verse*, 1964, translated by Geoffrey Bownas and Anthony Thwaite (*haiku* by Kobayashi Issa).

Richards Press Ltd.: *Kai Lung Unrolls His Mat*, 1942, by Ernest Bramah.

Secker & Warburg Ltd.: *The Biography of Franz Kafka*, 1947, by Max Brod, translated from the German by G. Humphreys Roberts.

Weidenfeld & Nicolson Ltd.: *Daily Life in Palestine at the Time of Christ*, 1962, by Daniel-Rops, translated from the French by Patrick O'Brian.

Other acknowledgments p. 179–180.

Introduction

It is a hard and difficult task to dispute with men's bellies

PLUTARCH

The reasons given for not adopting a vegetarian form of cookery are usually straightforward. Give up the pleasures of succulent meats for an interminable diet of nut rissoles and boiled vegetables? Even those with no gourmet pretensions may find this hard to stomach. But the disquiet which many feel about broiler factories and the intensive rearing of farm animals has brought about a widespread wish for some change of habit. So the problem becomes one of taste against conscience. Can the two ever be reconciled? I think they can—it is mainly why this book has been compiled.

Over the years of collecting, adapting and evolving recipes I became aware of a most interesting thing—the curious interchangeability of taste which some foods have with each other. Even those flavours we have long associated with meat or fish are not necessarily exclusive to them, but can be reproduced successfully in many different ways. For example, I have made squash or pumpkin taste like some exotic sea food, juicy "hamburgers" out of minced wheat gluten, and "shmaltz"—a Jewish delicacy—without resorting to chicken fat. This does not mean that all I am concerned with is imitating non-vegetarian flavours—far from it. For while these variations are fascinating in themselves, they only serve to point up what is obvious—that there is practically no limit to the variety of ways in which exciting new tastes can be achieved. On the other hand, a great many of the recipes which follow embody the traditional fare of many lands. So you will find anything from European and English casseroles to Asian and western soups, salads with intricate or simple dressings, appetizers and spreads of every description, Chinese crisp-fried vegetables, spicy felaffels, the mellow beauty of Arabic Im-Hasha, golden crusty pizzas, aromatic pillaus.

Too often, vegetarian cookery has meant vegetables with the meat left out—a fact which discourages all but the most rigid "principle-arians". I hope to show that there is nothing ascetic about such cookery; on the contrary, that there is no anomaly in being a vegetarian and a lover of good food at the same time! To produce, in short, stimulating meals on which a first class vintage wine will not be wasted.

A vegetarian diet can be not only healthful and sustaining, but, what is just as important, infinitely appetizing as well. Literally millions of people in India, China, Greece and the Balkans have eaten foods without either meat or fish in them for centuries. Culinary skills, developed through the ages, and embellished with regional herbs and spices, created a wealth of traditional dishes that were toothsome for peasant and king alike. The use of fresh green ginger, sweet coriander, soy sauce, sesame seeds, sea-salt and good wine vinegar can help us to re-create these dishes in our own kitchens.

Our task is made easier because of the exuberant variety of vegetables now available in this country, which gives us the opportunity of trying them out singly and in countless combinations. To name but a few: the shiny purple aubergine —which takes superbly to being marinated and charcoal-grilled on skewers—sweet green and red peppers, creamy avocados, fleshy globe artichokes, the slightly bitter batavia. To these we can add sun-scented herbs like dill, basil and lemon thyme; the many textures and tastes of green and black olives; pastas; grains particularly rich in minerals like millet and buckwheat; almonds, pistachios and pecans. None of these fall into the "exotic" category any more; today they can be found at many local stores.

The simplicity of our form of cookery makes little demand in the way of special kitchen utensils. A good heavy frying pan (stainless steel and copper-bottomed if possible), a small electric coffee-grinder for pulverizing nuts and grains (and coffee!), a mortar and pestle, a kitchen scale, a garlic press, a small hand mincer—these are basically the necessary equipment. Other than this, the recipes follow a simple underlying principle, the principle of most good cookery—to put a stress on what you use, but more on how you use it.

S.B.

Before you go further . . .

What follows is a list of some of the foods mentioned in this book that may be unfamiliar to readers. Here you will find a few introductory hints and ideas for using them, and details of their availability. Other perhaps "unfamiliar" foods are dealt with in the recipes where they occur.

Agar Agar A perfect substitute for gelatin, Agar Agar is derived from seaweed. Flavourless in itself, it has the advantage of dissolving quickly in water below the boiling point, so that in jelling fresh fruit juices few of the valuable vitamins are lost. Obtainable at health food stores and some pharmacists.

Almonds Are of course known to everyone, but mostly as a nut. Strictly speaking, according to some classifiers of the subject, they are a fruit. Almonds, unlike other nuts, have strong anti-acid properties, and can be adapted to use in an astonishing array of dishes both savoury and sweet. They are also rich in protein and minerals.

Aubergines or Eggplants These purple vegetables of the marrow family can be turned into gourmet fare by being barbecued, casseroled in wine, puréed for fritters, or smoked and chopped with fried onions and olive oil. They should be bought only when their skins are firm and shiny. Once the skin is dull, you can take it that the vegetable is old and will turn out disappointing.

Avocados At one time this fruit-vegetable was in the luxury class. Nowadays it is widely available and relatively inexpensive. It makes an ideal choice for picnics. Simply cut open lengthwise, remove the large stone and fill the hollows of each half with cottage cheese, chopped fresh herbs, sea-salt, sliced spring onions—and take along a container of your favourite salad dressing. Add French bread and wine and olives for a perfect alfresco meal. Use only ripened avocados. If they are hard when you buy them, allow them to ripen first. The ripening process can be speeded up by wrapping the fruit in a towel for several days. To test for ripeness, press the fruit gently with a thumb or forefinger. When the texture is like that of a fairly firm pillow, it is ready for eating.

Bean Sprouts   Bean sprouts are the white and tender, juicy and crunchy shoots of a small dry green pea called "moong" by Indians, and a host of other names by other peoples. Used principally in fried-stirred Chinese dishes, but can be adapted to many other combinations. A rich source of vitamins and minerals. The trouble is getting them fresh—and then they should be used within 24 hours. If you get the tinned variety you may wonder what I have been talking about, since they tend to be less tasty and crunchy, and it is advisable to crisp them up in several changes of very cold water. The fresh variety is delivered daily most of the year to Chinese food stores and some greengrocers.

Cheese   Just a few remarks. Since most cheeses are made with animal rennet (a preparation derived from the stomach milk of unweaned calves), it might be of interest to list a few which are naturally prepared:

Geska cheese—a Swiss product, also called Green Cheese or Schabsieger. Geska is made from skimmed cows' milk, to which the mountain herb "blue meliot" is added. It is a completely hard cheese, specifically meant for grating, and can be used in all cases where Parmesan is called for. Geska has a highly distinctive flavour.

Cottage cheese, cream cheese, creamery cheese, curd cheese— these are varieties of "soft" cheeses usually made without the addition of any rennet whatever.

Bryndza—a "soft" cheese derived from sheep's milk with a flavour remarkably like Gorgonzola. Hardens quickly after several days if kept cold. Used widely throughout central and Balkan Europe. An excellent variety from the mountains of Poland is available in Polish food stores. A Polish delicacy when combined with dill-pickled cucumbers.

Note   There are quite a few "hard" cheeses made without animal rennet, but these have so far not been identified with any exactitude. Probably, soon, such identifications will be made as experimentation with non-animal rennets—much of it highly successful—goes on.

Coriander   A most palatable plant of which both leaves and seeds are eaten. The leaves are used extensively in Indian curries and Greek vegetable salads. The seeds are indispensable for flavouring a wide variety of Mediterranean dishes, from the Maghreb to Provence to Cyprus; while the powder, which is the seed crushed fine, is also added to curries, or lentils, or the Moroccan speciality of grilled black olives and potatoes. In each of its forms, but mainly in the seed and powder, coriander has a mild aromatic quality that is most agreeable.

Courgettes   The French name for zucchini.

Demarara Sugar   Unrefined or raw sugar.

Elixir Végétal de la Grande Chartreuse   This delightful essence has been made since 1605, by the same monks who produce the liqueur Chartreuse. It is compounded of nearly 200 plants and mountain herbs steeped in a base of *eau de vie*. It is particularly good added to *tisanes*, especially lime-blossom; it imparts an unusual piquancy to fresh fruit drinks and fruit salads; it is delightful in cocktails. Only a few drops are needed. The Fathers of the Grande Chartreuse also claim for it*—among dozens of other uses—that it is effective in counteracting indigestion, sea-sickness and other forms of nausea.

Garlic   Probably the most essential flavouring there is. The unabashed taste has often frightened off its would-be lovers, but used correctly it is never offensive—quite the contrary. When garlic is added, even lavishly, to dishes which are to be cooked, *there is no strong smell*—only a harmonious development of the inherent flavours of the food it is being cooked with. Even when raw, as in that superb Provençal mayonnaise *aioli*, or in salad dressings, its stimulating presence need not deter you—a little parsley chewed afterwards will diminish the effect. The French variety is invariably best. In June you can enjoy a special treat with "fresh" garlic—this is when the garlic has been newly picked and its size, because of the high moisture content, is almost three to four times the usual one. It is particularly mild at this time.

---

* They claim it in writing only, of course, since Carthusians are vowed to strict silence—and an exclusively vegetarian diet.

Ginger, fresh (or green)   A root which assumes the weirdest shapes. Peeled and used sparingly, it imparts the quality of Chinese-ness to Chinese dishes and soups. Generally used less sparingly in Indian curries. Obtainable at Chinese and Indian provision stores and better fruiterers.

Herbs   Should never be used merely for decorative purposes. Besides their known therapeutic value, the addition of fresh (or dried) herbs—to a salad dressing, to steamed vegetables, soups, or even strewn thickly over plain bread and butter— embellishes the meanest food with sumptuousness. Without herbs many foods are simply uninteresting. With them, the gastric juices are stimulated and enjoyment is heightened. One could almost say the idea of good cookery is unthinkable without them. Below I list some of the herbs I have found most valuable.

Basil   exquisite and mildly piquant. Most acceptable, chopped, over tomato or cucumber slices, or macerated in a mortar and added to salad dressings. Perfect for mixing with soft cheese or sprinkling over bread and butter and lettuce sandwiches. Unfortunately, the season for basil is very short—late July to mid-August—but the dried variety put out by "Chiltern Herbs" is the next best thing.

Dill   in my own opinion, the most flavoursome of the herb family. Can be used lavishly over almost every savoury food imaginable. Unique when companied with cucumber or cold boiled potatoes and sour cream. Widely used in Scandinavia, central and eastern Europe—traditionally in pickling cucumbers and mushrooms. Dill first appears in the shops as a small rich-green shrub—at this stage its taste is almost too subtle. It is generally best when about 10 inches long. In its later stages it can reach as much as 2½ to 3 feet. When it is this size it is ideal for use in pickling. Or for drying. Or continued eating for that matter, and the yellow flowers should be used as well.

Borage   an almost melony-tasting herb with tiny pink or blue flowers—the whole plant is edible. It is best added to salads or to iced summer drinks like fresh lemon or lime juice.

Tarragon   a sprig of this kept in a bottle of good wine vinegar for a week will impart a zestful flavour to dressings of all kinds. Also very good chopped fine and sprinkled on raw cauliflower.

Parsley   needs no introduction, since it has long been a

favourite in English cookery In its lesser known guise it is an excellent breath deodorizer, especially after eating onions or garlic, or merely after smoking too much.

Thyme a strong-scented herb, thyme should be used rather sparingly. Adds a breath of strange fragrance to salad dressings.

If you can manage to get large bunches of fresh herbs at the time of year they are most plentiful, and therefore cheapest, hang them in a clean airy place till they are dry and crumbly. Then put them in jars, tightly stoppered, and you will be able to enjoy their fragrant use as long as they last.

Instant Soup A quite fabulous one is the one called "Snow-crest", a Swiss product of 100% vegetable origin. The "vege-table" origin is mentioned because, when made, it has the taste and appearance of chicken soup. It really is instant too—one simply adds $1-1\frac{1}{4}$ teaspoons of the soup powder to a cup of freshly boiled water and it is ready to serve. I have found it useful in a variety of ways—as "stock", as a less usual medium for cooking rice, as the basis for Chinese soups (Greens and Egg-Froth, White Mushroom and Ginger).
A very similar preparation, also Swiss, is "Morga Vegetable Bouillon", available at most health food counters.

Maple Syrup A sweetening agent with a spectacular taste—for flavouring pancakes, ice-cream, cereals, desserts, *pain perdu*, yoghourt. Distilled from the sap of a species of maple tree grown principally in Quebec and the northern New England states. It has an enchantingly mellow, velvety sweetness which is never cloying. Only "100% pure" is worth considering. Obtainable at better provision stores.

Matzo Meal A meal produced from crushing *matzo*, the Jewish unleavened bread. There are two kinds: medium and fine ground. Matzo meal is in many ways superior to flour for binding ingredients together with egg. Since it is already baked, it never has a "raw" taste, nor does it cause food to become stodgy or heavy. Particularly good as a basis for dumplings, or added to potato pancakes or gluten-burgers. When matzo meal is called for in any of the recipes, *fine ground only* is meant. Generally available.

Meatless Steaks A savoury product prepared from wheat

gluten, and available at all health food shops. Can be metamor-
phosed into a wide variety of delicious and substantial dishes
with the smallest amount of trouble. An ideal food, too, for
those who are slimming or want to stay slim—since it is rich in
protein but very low in calories.

Olive oil   There are so many varieties that it is sometimes
difficult to make a choice. Nevertheless, certain qualities are to
be looked for. Some olive oils are so distinguished that we may
associate them, not unworthily, with *grand cru* vintage wines.
Those that fall into this class are usually from Provence, and
are denoted "first cold pressing". Good Provençal olive oils are
characterized by their lightness and extreme subtlety of taste,
almost lack of it. They should be reserved for the occasions
where they really matter: in salad dressings, in *aiolis*, in
mayonnaise generally. You can be slightly less fussy when it
comes to olive oil for frying.

Peppers, sweet   Sweet green and red peppers should not be
confused with the smaller, pointed, hot green and red peppers
(chillies) which are used in Indian cookery and are very hot
indeed. The sweet variety are mild and juicy and add luscious
colour to salad plates. They take well to being stuffed and baked
or being pickled as a relish. The inner seeds should always be
removed before eating, as there is a chance of their being
somewhat hot.

Pickling Spice (mixed)   Contains, among other things, peppercorns, coriander and mustard seed, dried chilli peppers,
crumbled bay leaf, dried juniper berries, dried ginger. Essential for the preparation of dill pickled cucumbers (p. 65). Aside
from pickle solutions, however, it provides a subtle aromatic
backdrop to more exquisite dishes (see Mushroom Pâté).
Widely available.

Sea-salt   Which French cookery employs widely as *sel
marin*, far surpasses ordinary table salt in taste. Once you have
used a good sea-salt, you will find the other kind overly obvious
and bitter. The best sea-salt I have found is "Maldon", which is
drier than most other varieties, and crumbles easily without the
benefit of a salt mill. (N.B. Whenever salt is called for in a

recipe, *the use of sea-salt is specified.* If you wish to substitute ordinary table salt in any of the dishes, you will have to cut down on the amount of sea-salt indicated and adjust to your own taste.)

Seaweed In a country like Japan, traditionally meagre in the produce of the soil, the role of seaweed in the national diet has been a sustaining one. Mean fare it may be considered—so were potatoes for many centuries—but the beauty of it is its delightful "sea-food" taste, aside from rich mineral qualities. There are two kinds generally available: *Konbu* which is flat and broad, and *Iziki*, which looks like tangled vermicelli. Obtainable: health food stores and foreign or specialty food shops.

Sesame seeds The seeds of a sub-tropical plant whose mild, nut-like flavour lends itself to dishes both savoury and sweet. Very pleasant as a topping for biscuits, bread and pastry, and as the basis for many oriental sweetmeats. As a condiment: toasted and ground with sea-salt and added to dishes like fried-stirred vegetables and rice. Sesame seeds are rich in Vitamin B complex. Available: Greek, Italian, Spanish and Indian provision stores. Ready toasted sesame seeds obtainable at health food stores and specialty food shops.

Soy sauce One of the most superior seasonings there is. Primarily used in Chinese and Japanese dishes, to produce the delightful thin brown gravy; or with meals, as a savoury "dip". Soy sauce is exceedingly versatile, and enlivens the appeal of western as well as eastern cookery. It is ideal for adding to marinades, soups, omelettes, even to Indian curries. The strange thing about it is its protean quality: in Chinese dishes it establishes the Chinese-ness of taste; in Russian casseroles it gives an undeniably "Russian" flavour. There are several qualities of Chinese soy sauce widely available. There is also a Japanese variety—Kikkoman—which surpasses any other for dipping purposes: now widely available in supermarkets as well as health food stores and specialty shops.

Tisanes In France, after you've eaten too lavishly, the usual thing is to call for a *tisane.* And if it's a *tilleul* (lime-blossom), you're bound to add a few drops of *Elixir Végétal* to it. Tisanes are blossom-teas prepared simply in the manner of ordinary tea.

What makes them interesting is that they tend to soothe the digestive and nervous systems (so tisane-users always claim), as well as having other healthful properties. The taste for blossom-teas must often be acquired. Once acquired, you will even find them an excellent sometime substitute for breakfast drinking.

Lime-blossom   one of the most delightful and fragrant of all blossom-teas. A good one to begin with. (Used by some Persians as a "green tea", unsweetened.)

Camomile   very subtle flavour, alleged to be soothing to the gastro-intestinal tract.

Rose-hip   an excellent source of Vitamin C—think of it when next you have the misery of a feverish cold. Very full-bodied "rosy" taste. Rose-hips are prized in eastern Europe for making jams and syrups.

Lemon-blossom   redolent of lemony fragrance. Said to be soporific in effect, therefore recommended to insomniacs. Very pleasant mixed in equal proportions with lime-blossom.

England

To bend with apples the moss'd cottage-trees,
And fill all fruit with ripeness to the core;
To swell the gourd, and plump the hazel shells
With a sweet kernel; to set budding more,
And still more, later flowers for the bees . . .

KEATS (*To Autumn*)

And if, in our more industrial age, these lines seem better attuned to the dewy visions of Romantic poets, it is only because most men's and poets' interests have shifted elsewhere meantime. But to those who know it, the richness of the English harvest is still an ebullience of cereals, fruits, vegetables, nuts and honey.

We have been told that before the First War English apples were considered a delicacy in Russia. "Apples to Russia?" you will say—in much the same way that you might say "salt to Siberia?" But, if you do, you will be overlooking Russian taste sense, which is very good. The test of an apple in those days was not only for flavour but for whether it "spurted"—spurted when you bit in it. And for this many English apples qualify, especially in their season, which is the time to eat them . . . The Cox's Orange Pippin, with its taste like new wine in a fruit jacket, the tart and rosy Beauty of Bath, the D'Arcy Spice, with its deep subtleties, the fragrant Egremont Russet, the Worcester Pearmain. When autumn comes it's time to try them all, including the sturdy Bramley—in pies, tarts, compotes and puddings; and the others in salads or munched as they are. In some of the following recipes you will find this autumnal variety put to use, in cooked dishes and raw.

HONEY PEARS

Peel firm but ripe **pears**—Comice if they're available. Core from stems downwards, thoroughly, but not through the bottoms.

Fill hollows with a mixture of: **1 oz. fresh ground almonds**

(put through your electric grinder), $1\frac{1}{2}$ **tbs. mild honey, 1
tbs. minced seedless raisins** (first plumped in hot water for
7–10 minutes), a pinch of **cinnamon.** Enough to fill 3 large or
4 medium size pears.

Stand pears upright in a well buttered casserole. Dot pears
with more **butter,** drizzle over lightly with **honey.** Bake,
uncovered, in a slow oven (325°—Gas 3) for about 40 minutes,
or till pears are glazed-looking and very tender. Serve hot or
chilled with **thin cream.**

APPLE BEETS

Choose **3–4 round beetroots** (raw)—enough to fill comfortably a medium size casserole.

Peel and take thin slices off the tops. Hollow out carefully,
making cavities as large as possible without cutting through—
leave approximately a $\frac{1}{2}$-inch thickness. Use scooped out parts
in vegetable soup.

In **1 tbs. olive oil** fry: $2\frac{1}{2}$ **oz. chopped sweet onion, 1
stalk (1 oz.) celery** chopped fine, **1 crushed garlic clove.**
Fry 3–4 minutes. Add **7 oz. tart apple,** peeled and thin-sliced,
$4\frac{1}{2}$ **tsp. demerara sugar.** Stir, cover, simmer till apples are
completely soft. Put mixture into a bowl and let cool. Then
blend with $\frac{3}{4}$ **tsp. sea-salt** and $\frac{3}{4}$ **cup fresh bread-crumbs.**

Stuff mixture into hollowed out beetroots, replace tops,
arrange in an oiled casserole. Sprinkle beets with sea-salt,
drizzle with more olive oil. Pour the juice of $\frac{1}{2}$ **lemon** and $\frac{1}{4}$ **cup
water** into the casserole.

Bake at 325° (Gas 3) for about 2 hours, or till beetroots are
tender. Cut into thick rounds. Serve with **baked potatoes** and
plain **lettuce salad.** (4)

LITTLE GEM GRILLS

The small round **gourds** called Little Gems are generally
available in late summer. It could be said that what *Charentais*
are to the world of melons, Little Gems are to the world of
gourds. One of the easiest and pleasantest ways of making them
is simply to cut each in half crosswise, remove the seeds (they
can be used very effectively for Chew-Strew, see p. 82), spread
the cut surfaces with **butter,** a small amount of **chopped
tarragon, sea-salt,** and grill for 15–30 minutes, or till tender.
Then sprinkle over with a little fresh **lemon juice** and serve
hot—with **Grated Potato Pudding** and **Pickled Salad.**

Variation: Fill the hollows and rub round the rims of each Little Gem half with **1-1½ tsp. Herb Butter:** Cream **2 tbs. butter** together with **½ tsp. dry crumbled dill, ½ tsp. dry crumbled oregano** or **marjoram, ½ tsp. sea-salt.** Blend well and chill till needed. (Enough for 2-3 medium size Little Gems.)

GREEN SIMMER

A very "haunting" and healthful delicacy.

Wash thoroughly **2 good sized bunches of fresh watercress.** Cut away the tough stems. Shake as dry as possible. Chop roughly.

Melt **3 tbs. butter** in a heavy saucepan over a low heat. When butter begins to froth add the watercress. Cover the pan and simmer 10 minutes. Season with **1 tsp. sea-salt,** re-cover pan, continue simmering till tender—about 10-20 minutes longer. Add a squeeze of fresh **lemon juice,** mix through, serve hot. Enough for 2. (See p. 167 for elaboration.)

MUSHROOM MAIZE CASSEROLE

Lightly fry **1 oz. chopped onion** in **1 tbs. butter** for 3 minutes. Then add: **4 oz. fine sliced mushrooms, 2½ tsp. soy sauce, 2 oz. cucumber** peeled and sliced. Fry and stir another 3 minutes.

Transfer to a casserole (1½ pint), add **¼ cup buttermilk, 1 tsp. sea-salt,** a pinch of fresh ground **pepper, 3-4 tbs. raw patna rice, 1 small packet frozen kernel corn (5 oz.).** Mix through and sprinkle over with **½ tsp. dry crumbled dill.** Cover and bake in a medium oven (350°—Gas 4) for 40 minutes. (3-4)

Serve with **Fruited Cabbage Salad**—see below.

EGGS IN ALE

"One egg broken into a pint of good ale and brewed well together, and eaten with bread, makes a brave meal." So says Thos. Tryon,* and quite truthfully. Tryon was a 17th century English food reformer, whose works influenced Benjamin Franklin to adopt a vegetarian diet in his younger days; to this diet Franklin avowed all his future success in life. Tryon's Eggs in Ale makes an extremely invigorating breakfast or

* In *Bill of Fare* (*Wisdom's Dictates: or, Aphorisms & Rules, Physical, Moral and Divine*), London, 1691.

lunch—but a ½ pint of ale will do, or **1 pint ale** will brew **2-3 eggs** quite nicely.

Simply heat good ale to boiling point, savour the "hoppy" smell if you like, make a whirlpool, proceed as for poached eggs. Skim out and serve on rounds of **buttered toast.** There will be a very lovely ale-like taste to the eggs.

THREE GREENS BOIL

Another of Tryon's recipes, which is "a friendly, exhilarating food, generating good blood and fine spirits . . ."

Simmer ½ **lb. well washed spinach** (heavy stems removed) together with ½ **lb. curly endive,** and a bunch of young **parsley** in very little water till tender (not more than 15-20 minutes). Drain well, add **butter** and **sea-salt,** toss through, serve immediately with **wholemeal bread and butter** and glasses of **ale.** (Serves 4)

EGGS AND VINEGAR

The third of Tryon's simple but wholesome recipes goes as follows.

Beat **eggs** together and prepare omelettes in the usual manner, or just break eggs into frothing simmering butter, cover pan, cook gently 5-6 minutes.

Meanwhile, melt more **butter**—about **2 tsp. per egg**— and stir in a goodly amount of **wine vinegar.** Mix till well infused. Then serve the eggs, pour the mixture immediately over, add a sprinkle of **sea-salt** and eat.

According to Tryon, the butter/vinegar mixture makes the eggs "lighter and easier of digestion"—and certainly more delicious too. Accompany again with **buttered wheaten bread, spring onions,** and **cold ale.**

"Eat by season" is a thrifty proverb—don't look for delicacies at out-of-season times. But eating by season has another important virtue which implies—take advantage of fruits and vegetables when you can get them fresh, and use them in that way to preserve all their goodness and flavour. Raw salads are not only suitable for warm summer days; their high mineral and vitamin content makes them a necessary part—some would say *the* part—of at least one daily meal, summer *and* winter. Here are a few more unusual ways of serving them.

FRUITED CABBAGE SALAD

Prepare

6 oz. savoy cabbage—wash well, remove tough ribs, slice fine

1 medium size pear or peach—peel, cut flesh into small cubes

6 large grapes—cut in halves, seed, divide into quarters

1 tsp. seedless raisins—cut in halves

½ oz. hazelnuts and almonds—blanch, skin, shred

2 tbs. watercress leaves—chop coarsely

1 fresh mint leaf—chop fine

Place ingredients in a salad bowl and make up a dressing: **1½ tbs. olive oil, 2 tsp. lemon juice, 1 tsp. mild honey, ½ tsp. sea-salt, 1 tsp. water, 1½ tsp. cream, 1 tsp. wine vinegar.** Stir and mix till well amalgamated, pour into the salad. Toss lightly but thoroughly.

Allow salad to stand 10–15 minutes before serving. (4)

CHICORY AND PLUM SALAD

Wash **2 medium size heads of chicory,** shake dry, remove wilted or discoloured leaves. Cut into ½-inch rounds, separate into rings.

Wash and stone **4–5 sweet purple plums,** cut into quarters.

Arrange plums and chicory in individual bowls over leaves of **lettuce.** Sprinkle over with this dressing: **3 tbs. buttermilk, 1 tbs. wine vinegar, 2 tsp. demerara sugar, ½ tsp. sea-salt, ¼ tsp. fresh grated lemon rind.** (4)

HUGUENOT SOUP

The Huguenots came with many skills, not least the one for making foods tasty. Here is a simple soup to make with very plain ingredients, but follow the simple scheme below and see how it produces an elegant flavour.

Bring lightly salted water to boil in a large saucepan (an inch of water). Add **1 lb. potatoes** peeled and small-diced, and **1 small chopped onion (2–3 oz.).** Cook gently, covered, till potatoes are tender. Add **4 cups milk,** bring slowly back to the boil, let it barely simmer.

Meanwhile, in a heavy frying pan, gently heat up **1 oz. sifted plain flour.** Stir frequently till flour takes on a very pale golden colour. Then blend in **2 tbs. butter** and continue stirring over the same low heat till mixture browns—but doesn't burn! Add immediately to the soup, stir through, and continue stirring and simmering till soup thickens somewhat—about 5 minutes. Add **4 tsp. sea-salt,** and a little fresh ground black **pepper** if you like, and serve.

Sprinkle the surface of each soup bowl with a small handful of **chopped watercress.** (4)

Follow with Mixed Fritters.

MIXED FRITTERS

Collect together and wash **2 oz. young green beans, a small head of cauliflower (about 8 oz.), 2 stalks of celery.** Parboil in a large saucepan of salted water. Drain, cool. Cut beans in halves and celery in short sections, break cauliflower into flowerets and cut into medium thick slices. Separate the **heart of a crisp lettuce** into leaves, wash, shake dry, set aside.

Heat **deep oil** in a saucepan.

Prepare a batter: Sieve **1 cup plain flour** into a bowl, add **2 eggs, 2 tsp. sea-salt, 1 tbs. olive oil, ½ cup water, 4–5 chopped fresh mint leaves.** Mix lightly together.

When oil is sufficiently hot, dip *parboiled* vegetables into batter, fry till rich golden on all sides. Drain, salt lightly, keep warm. Now take up the lettuce leaves, 2 at a time, lay them flat against each other, dip in the batter and fry till light golden on each side. (The lettuce fritters should emerge with the fried batter taking the pattern of the enclosed leaves.) Drain, salt and serve all together (enough for 4) with a Pickled Salad.

PICKLED SALAD

Slice **6 large tomatoes** into quarters, mix with **12 pickled onions** cut in halves, **2 tbs. diced pickled walnuts, 4 chopped pickled gherkins.** Dress with **salad cream** thinned down with a little plain **yoghourt.**

ASPARAGUS AND POTATOES

In a baking dish arrange a thick layer of **asparagus,** fresh-cooked or tinned. Sprinkle over generously with cut pieces of **butter** and a little crumbled **sage.** Drizzle over with **lemon juice,** season with **sea-salt.**

Top up with **mashed seasoned potatoes** and bake—uncovered—at 375° (Gas 5) for 45 minutes, or till potatoes are crusted and golden.

WINTER RICE SALAD

Cook ¾ **cup (6 oz.) washed patna rice** in approximately **1 cup water** as for dry-cooked rice (see p. 89). Steam as usual, then cool. Put in a large bowl and add: a scant ½ **tsp. dry crumbled borage, 2 oz. shredded carrot, 1 oz. shredded raw beetroot** or **fine sliced raw cauliflower, a small handful of lightly toasted sunflower seeds, 1 tsp. lemon juice, 1 tbs. olive oil,** ½–¾ **tsp. sea-salt** and a dash of **pepper.** (3) Serve with Almond Bake (p. 162).

STUFFED MANGOES

A very unusual and lusty variation on pickled cucumbers, as practised in Elizabethan times—first Elizabethan times, of course.

Take small *firm* **ridge cucumbers** (available August/September), slice off one end of each. Carefully core out a little of the centre nearly all the way through—don't come out the other end. Fill up with a mixture of fine-chopped **garlic,** bits of **fresh horseradish** and **fresh ginger,** a little **mustard seed.** (Yes, your ancestors used all these, but maybe you prefer to doubt it, to see it as a "gift", rather, from Russia to England—a recipe perhaps handed to Elizabeth's ambassador at the Kremlin by Tsar Ivan the Terrible?) Fasten ends back on with toothpicks, then set cucumbers upright—and snugly together—in a sufficiently deep earthenware crock. Make up a pickle solution: For every pint of **white vinegar** add **4 tsp. sea-salt, 3 whole cloves,** a good sized **bay-leaf.** Bring to the boil in a saucepan, simmer 7 minutes, cool, pour over the cucumbers, seeing that they're well immersed. Cover securely, leave for 1 week to pickle. Sample and eat.

SHREDDED CELERY-LOVAGE APPETIZER

Trim and clean **5 good sized stalks of celery,** discard leaves. Cut stalks in half, parboil for 4 minutes, drain, plunge into icy water—2 changes of icy water if necessary—till celery is cold. Drain again, then slice into 2 inch sections, and sliver lengthwise into thin sticks. Arrange in a shallow bowl, cover over with this dressing: 1½ **tbs. olive oil,** 1½ **tsp. lemon juice, 1 tsp. wine vinegar,** ½ **tsp. demerara sugar,** ¾–1 **tsp. sea-salt,** all well amalgamated, then mixed through with **6–7 leaves of fresh lovage** chopped up.

Serve immediately, or soon after, unaccompanied except for bread or bread sticks. (4)

PICKLED WALNUT SAUCE

Sieve **6 whole pickled walnuts** into a small bowl. Add **4 tbs. olive oil** and stir through well, then **2 tsp. lemon juice** and stir again. Then **1 tsp. sea-salt, 2 tbs. fine minced spring onion, 2 tbs. dry bread-crumbs** (untoasted). Beat well together and let stand for 15 minutes before serving, or till crumbs have liquefied.

A very delightful "dip" for toasted bread chunks, or as a spread over bread, or with boiled new potatoes, or in the hollows of celery stalks. (3–4)

GRATED POTATO PUDDING

Grate very fine **1½ lb. peeled potatoes.** Squeeze out all the liquid—this is important. Do it by putting the grated potato into a sieve and pressing with the back of a wooden spoon, or any other way your ingenuity leads you. Put the grated potato into a bowl. Add to it: **1 small minced onion, 1 small grated carrot, 2 tsp. sea-salt,** a pinch of **pepper, 2 small eggs, 6 tbs. plain flour.** Blend very well together, add **1 tbs. olive oil,** blend again.

Oil a 1½ pint glass casserole, pile the potato mixture into it, level the surface lightly. Bake, uncovered, in a moderate oven (375°—Gas 5) for 50 minutes to 1 hour, or till top and sides are crisp and brown. Serve hot with a large raw salad—**Fruited Cabbage Salad** would be nice. (3–4)

CUCUMBER BUTTER

Algernon: Please don't touch the cucumber sandwiches. They are ordered specially for Aunt Augusta (*takes one and eats it*).
Jack: Well, you have been eating them all the time.
Algernon: That is quite a different matter.

WILDE (*The Importance of Being Earnest*)

... And so is cucumber butter quite a different matter from slices of cucumber over bread, though the taste retains the same quality of fresh greenness, but is made bolder—with a piquancy of lemon and tanginess of mint; and mellower—in a creaminess of butter. A good way of giving distinction to the sometimes very pallid, very undistinguished tasting cucumbers we get nowadays.

Grate **6 oz. unpeeled cucumber** very fine. Squeeze all the liquid out. Mix grated cucumber with **2 tbs. lemon juice,**

1 tsp. **sea-salt, 2 fresh mint leaves** chopped fine. Work in **4 tbs. softened butter** and blend till smooth. Chill till firm again. Spread over **thin slices of white bread,** crusts removed, roll up and fasten with cocktail picks. Or serve over **melba toast.** (4)

LITTLE CLOTTED CREAM GATEAUX

Another somewhat effete preparation—like cucumber butter sandwich rolls—but, like so many effete things, tempting and delicious all the same. And if, like Wilde, you can resist everything except temptation, these are the logical things for your next high tea.

Have ready a packet of thin, very crisp, good quality **sweet biscuits.**

Mix **6 tbs. curd** or **farmers' cheese** with **6 tbs. clotted cream** and **4 tbs. soft light-brown sugar** (tamped down). Beat together till light and creamy.

Allow 5–6 biscuits for each "gateau". Spread a small amount of the cream mixture over all of them but one. Then sprinkle over the creamed biscuits: a fine layer of **crushed walnuts,** a few drops of **brandy** (optional). Layer them up evenly, top with the plain biscuit. Wrap each "gateau" in aluminium foil securely, put into the freezer compartment of your refrigerator. Leave till next day or till the biscuits have softened and become one in texture with the rest of the filling. (8 "gateaux")

PANCAKES AND PANCAKE VARIATIONS

Use your favourite pancake formula or this one:

4 oz. plain flour, 2 eggs, 1 tbs. olive oil, ⅛ tsp. sea-salt, 1 cup milk. Sieve flour and salt into a bowl, make a well in the centre. Drop the eggs in, stir through the flour. Add the oil, mix again, and the milk, slowly. Blend lightly till you have a smooth batter. Let it stand for half-an-hour before using. (Enough for 16 pancakes)

Make up a quantity of pancakes on a lightly buttered griddle —baked to rich golden on the first side, and 15–20 seconds on the other. Arrange fillings on the *well-baked side*.

Sweet Fillings

Peach-almond Cut peeled ripe **peaches** into very small pieces. Sprinkle over with **sugar** and **ground toasted almonds.** Spread over the pancakes, roll up, arrange in a shallow oven-proof dish. Dust with more ground almonds and sugar, heat for a few minutes under the grill.

Apple-cinnamon   Mix **applesauce** with **cinnamon** and **sugar** and a few **raisins** (plumped in freshly boiled water for 7–10 minutes). Spread over the pancakes, fold up—in envelope fashion—sprinkle with more cinnamon and sugar. Heat through in oven. Serve with thin cream.

Banana-orange   Mash ripe **bananas** till creamy, flavour with a little **orange juice** and fine grated **orange rind,** sprinkle with **sugar.** Spread over pancakes, roll up tightly, arrange in a shallow casserole dish. Sprinkle with more sugar, a few drops of **brandy.** Heat under the grill for a few minutes.

Savoury Fillings

Curd cheese and onion   Mix **curd cheese** with a little **cream** till smooth. Add a small amount of **fried onion rings,** some **salt** and **pepper.** Fill pancakes, roll up, arrange side by side in an oven dish. Dot with **butter,** dust with dry crumbled **marjoram.** Heat in a hot oven for 7–10 minutes.

Sweet corn and mint   Cook a small packet of **frozen sweet corn** till tender. Drain, season with **sea-salt, pepper,** a little **butter,** and a little chopped **fresh mint.** Spread over the pancakes, fold up, place in an oven dish. Dot with butter, heat through in the oven. Serve sprinkled over with **lemon juice.**

Asparagus-chervil   Mix, and heat in a little **butter, tender asparagus** (fresh-cooked or tinned) with a small handful of chopped **fresh chervil.** Arrange over pancakes, sprinkle with **olive oil, lemon juice, sea-salt.** Fold up, dot with butter, heat through in oven about 10 minutes.

Mushroom-walnut   Fry and stir in frothing **butter** fine-chopped **mushrooms,** a little chopped **onion,** some coarse-crushed **walnuts.** Fry a few minutes, season with sea-salt and pepper. Mix through, fry a minute longer. Fill pancakes, roll up, arrange in oven dish, dot with butter, grill till golden.

For everything that lives is holy,
life delights in life.

BLAKE (*America*)

Italy

It is also by no means destitute of a certain
voluptuousness, of an elegant and even
splendid luxury, if we employ curiosity
and art in the choice of the best fresh
vegetables ...

ANTONIO COCCHI (August, 1743)

The learned Doctor Cocchi, keeper of the Grand Duke of
Tuscany's museum, friend of Horace Walpole, surgeon and
scientist, was proclaiming here the merits of the Pythagorean
Diet. We do not know what reaction his hearers gave him on
that undoubtedly hot August day in Florence, but we do know
that the discourse was printed and circulated widely, and
translated into English in 1745.

Pythagoras, of course, was probably the most magnetic
"food-reforming" vegetarian who ever lived. It was said of him
that he merely used to fix his eye, open his silver mouth, and
whole villages were swept away in enthusiasm. But modern
man requires more convincing ...

FINOCCHIO DEL PADRONE

After removing all the feathery leaves and cleaning well,
slice **4 oz. fennel root** into very thin strips, lengthwise.

Cut **3 peeled shallots** into fine rings. Shred about **1 oz.
cos lettuce** coarsely. Chop fine **1 tbs. sweet red pepper**.

Heat **1 tbs. olive oil** in a heavy pan. Fry the shallots lightly
till softened but not coloured, together with ¼ **tsp. cummin
seed.** Add the red pepper, fennel slices, lettuce, ½ **tsp. sea-salt,
1-2 crushed garlic cloves.** Stir through and continue frying
over a low heat for 5 minutes. Stir again, occasionally. Now
pour in **3 tbs. buttermilk,** shake the pan to distribute, cover,
simmer till fennel is tender, about 12–15 minutes.

Beat **2 eggs** well, together with 1½ **tbs. matzo meal** and **1
rounded tsp. sea-salt.**

Remove cover from pan carefully, shake off any moisture

which may have collected. Raise heat slightly and pour eggs over. Cover pan again, continue cooking gently till eggs are nicely set.

When set, cut omelette in two, turn out on warmed plates, underside up. Serve with **lemon quarters,** bread, chilled white wine. (Serves 2)

PASTAS

Innumerable are the forms of pasta, and seemingly endless the imagination of Italian pasta makers. Every kind of knot, spiral, twist and cone, shell, cartwheel, skein and tube that ingenious hands can fashion from flour, water and eggs has been devised by them. Some types are reserved for special occasions, most others for everyday fare. And there is no reason to stick either to straight spaghetti or macaroni. All pastas can be delicious and varied in flavour—it all depends on the sauce they are bathed in to give them distinctive appeal.

Whichever one you use, it is always advisable to cook it in a large saucepan, in plenty of lightly salted water, so that there's ample room for it to move about in. And pastas are at their best when they are cooked till *just* tender, so that one's teeth have something to get into—a texture *al dente,* Italians call it.

Allow **3 oz. pasta** per person. When it is cooked, drain it thoroughly, add a nut of **butter,** stir to melt, pour over with the sauce you have chosen. Serve with bowls of **salad.**

WINE AND BLACK OLIVE SAUCE

A very rich, almost "antique" tasting sauce, that transforms spaghetti into a party affair.

Prepare

6 oz. tomato—peeled, cored, finely chopped
1½ oz. (after stoning) bland black olives—put through mincer
2 oz. onion—finely chopped
1 tbs. celery leaves—finely chopped

Heat **1 tbs. olive oil** in a small earthenware casserole, cook onions gently till mellowing and almost golden. Add **2 (or more) crushed cloves of garlic,** cook 2 minutes more—but don't let garlic brown. Now add the tomatoes, black olives, celery leaves. Sprinkle with **1½ tsp. sea-salt, 2 tsp. demerara sugar,** a pinch of dry crumbled **oregano.** Stir through, simmer slowly for 10 minutes. Now add ¾ **cup dry red wine,** bring to a light boil, return to a simmer. Continue cooking for about an hour, stirring from time to time. Then sieve thoroughly, discarding anything left behind. Pour sauce over hot buttered pasta, reheat through slightly and serve. (4)

TOMATO TWO PEPPERS SAUCE

Prepare
> **7-8 oz. tomato**—peeled, cored, finely chopped
> **a small onion (1 oz.)**—chopped fine
> ½ **oz. sweet green pepper**—minced
> ½ **oz. sweet red pepper**—minced
> **1 tsp. fine chopped fennel weed**—(optional)

Heat 1½ **tbs. olive oil** in a heavy saucepan. Fry onions till softened and just verging on the golden. Add **2 (or more) crushed cloves of garlic,** fry a minute or two, follow with the remaining vegetables, plus **1½–2 tsp. sea-salt, 1 rounded tsp. demerara sugar.** Stir, fry gently for 15 minutes. Pour in a cup of cold water, bring to the boil, then reduce to a simmer. Cook about 1½ hours. Sieve thoroughly. Return to pan and reheat, pour over hot buttered pasta. (4)

TOMATO HOT SAUCE

Peel, core and chop ¾ **lb. ripe tomatoes.**

Pulverize in a mortar **1–2 dried red chilli peppers** (seeded), together with **1 tsp. sea-salt.** Add a crumbling of dry or a sprinkling of fresh **mint** and amalgamate. Then **3 crushed garlic cloves** and pestle till smooth. Finally, **1 tbs. lemon juice** and amalgamate again.

In a small heavy saucepan heat ¼ **cup olive oil** together with ¼ **tsp. cummin seed.** Add the tomatoes and the "hot sauce". Stir well and simmer, over a low heat, for 45 minutes to 1 hour. (3)

PESTO

There are many variations of Pesto sauce, each employing cheese. Here is one with Geska:

Grind in a mortar to a fine green powder ½ **tsp. dry basil** together with ¾ **tsp. sea-salt.** When really fine, add in **1 tbs. grated Geska cheese** and grind again. Then another tbs. Geska cheese and repeat. Then **2 tsp. pine kernels,** which will create a slightly sticky mass, but grind as fine as possible. Add

1 crushed clove of garlic, pound and blend. Then the juice of a medium size **lemon,** which will liquefy and loosen everything. Finally, stir in **4 tbs. olive oil** in a thin steady stream, stirring very rapidly. The result should have the appearance of a lovely green cream. But even if a little less than completely creamy-looking, the taste is still superb.

The Genoese custom is to have a few **boiled potato slices** on top of the pasta, then the sauce poured over all. Enough for 2–3 with or without the potatoes.

GREEN SAUCE

Another green sauce, but deeper and richer in colour, deriving its greenness from a copious mixture of herbs.

Pulverize in a mortar: ½ **tsp. dry oregano, 1 tsp. dry basil,** ½ **tsp. sea-salt.** Pulverize to powder. Turn powder out of mortar on to a plate.

Now grind 1½ **tsp. fresh parsley** in the mortar together with ½ **tsp. sea-salt,** after which add: **1 tsp. capers**—washed in water, squeezed dry, then minced, plus **a small crushed clove of garlic.** Blend well together. Add now **1 tbs. fine minced onion.** Return the dry herb powder to the mortar. Pound and amalgamate everything together. Follow with **4 tbs. olive oil,** bit by bit, stirring and working the residue off the sides into the centre of the mortar. Finish with **1 tbs. lemon juice** or **wine vinegar,** and blend in rapidly.

Pour over hot buttered pasta, heat through, serve with a sprinkling of **grated Geska.** (2–3)

Note: For convenience, sauces can be made in advance of using, then stored in the refrigerator for a few hours. The intensity of flavour of all the above sauces, with the possible exception of Tomato Two Peppers, is such that only a small quantity is needed for each serving of pasta.

Very frequently, Italians don't bother with sauces at all. They merely pile a few vegetables on top of the pasta and add a few olives or capers. A rather pleasant one along this style is:

RED PEPPER PASTA

Wash **1 large or 2 small sweet red peppers,** slit open, remove seeds and pith, cut into 1 inch squares.

Lightly squeeze dry **2 tbs. capers.** Stone **6 black olives,** cut into halves.

Heat **2 tbs. olive oil** in a heavy pan, add the pepper squares, capers and olives. Cook over a gentle heat till peppers begin to soften and mellow. Turn frequently. Serve over hot buttered pasta. Sprinkle with **grated Geska.** (Serves 2)

MIXED SALAD

Besides being delicious and invigorating, salads are one of the most perfect regulators of bodily weight. Nimble rabbits have been advertising this fact for generations. In Italy, where pasta is consumed in such quantity, the population is still generally slim. The answer? Salads. Genial Italians, when they know each other well, will reproach their friends who do not conform to the national standard—they will say, "You should eat more salad". As a rule, Italians at home will eat salad in proportion to their pasta. A cauldron of noodles will be balanced by a similarly prodigious amount of lettuce. But this exuberance for salad does not confine itself to greens—more often the contrary. From a people who instilled the meaning of colour into art we expect more, and they don't disappoint us. Salads in Italy are usually colourful affairs of many mixed vegetables, with a smooth but tangy dressing. Here is an example:

Prepare

1 firm head of lettuce—washed, shaken dry, half left in leaves, half torn in large pieces
2 large tomatoes—cut into eighths
$\frac{1}{2}$ **cucumber**—sliced into rounds
$\frac{1}{4}$ **cup fresh young peas**
1 small cooked beetroot—cut into dice
1 handful of small radishes—left whole

Make a dressing

by grinding in a mortar—a scant $\frac{1}{2}$ **tsp. dry basil, 1 tsp. demerara sugar, 1 tsp. sea-salt.** Then add: **4 tbs. olive oil, 2 tbs. wine vinegar.** Blend.

Toss all the vegetables—except the tomatoes and lettuce leaves—in the dressing. Arrange the lettuce leaves in individual bowls, fill up with the dressed vegetables, distribute the tomato sections on top. (5–6)

FENNEL SALAD

As an appetizer or accompaniment to a pasta dinner . . .

Trim **2 medium size fennel roots (6 oz.)**, discarding all the tough outer leaves and all but 1 or 2 of the feathery stems. Slice roots into razor thin rounds, bathe in a dressing compounded of the following:

3 tbs. olive oil, 2 tbs. lemon juice, 1 tbs. wine vinegar, a pinch of **dry crumbled thyme, 1½ tsp. sea-salt, 1 tsp. honey.** Shake together in a closed bottle till emulsified, pour over the fennel. Chop the feathery fennel stem(s), sprinkle over the top. Allow to marinate 1–2 hours. (4)

ANTIPASTO

One of the most delightful of mixed salad matters is Antipasto, a choice selection of fresh cut vegetables allowed to mellow in a discreet marinade. On the principle that everything made at home is usually better, and tastier, the following recipe holds true—even if it doesn't compare in appearance with those beautiful arrangements put up so artfully in glass jars.

Prepare

> **2 oz. button mushroom caps**—remove stalks (and set aside for other purposes), cut caps in half
>
> **1 oz. young green beans**—cut in 1-inch sections
>
> **6 small pickling onions**—peeled but left whole
>
> **2 stalks celery (heart)**—cut in half, then in strips, but not too fine
>
> **1 oz. sweet green pepper flesh**—cut in small squares
>
> **1 oz. sweet red pepper flesh**—as preceding
>
> **½ oz. walnut halves**
>
> **4 oz. fresh white cauliflower**—cut in fairly thin floweret strips
>
> **1 small carrot (1 oz.)**—cut into matchstick strips

Arrange the vegetables in a small deep earthenware crock.

Make a marinade

> **¾ cup wine vinegar**
>
> **2½ tsp. sea-salt**
>
> **1 clove garlic**—sliced thin
>
> **⅛ tsp. dry crumbled oregano**
>
> **a small bunch of fresh borage**—chopped
>
> **1 tbs. fine chopped parsley**
>
> **a small piece of fennel weed** (optional)

a pinch of caraway seed
1½ tbs. demerara sugar

Pour the marinade into a small saucepan, bring to the boil. Cool. Transfer to a glass bottle. Add **5 tbs. olive oil.** Cap the bottle, shake vigorously till everything is emulsified. Pour the marinade over the cut vegetables. Cover the crock. Leave in a cool place for 8 hours at least—or make in the morning to serve in the evening. Stir the vegetables from time to time so that they're well coated in the marinade. If left to the following day they will be more richly flavoured, and even more richly flavoured on the third day. Serve as a pre-meal appetizer, arranged colourfully on a large platter, with some white Chianti or dry light sherry, and *grissini*—the thin sticks of crisp bread sold at all Italian and most continental food stores. Let everyone help themselves. Or save it for your family, as a wonderfully hearty breakfast. (Serves 4)

GREEN PEPPERS AND POTATOES

Char **2 small sweet green peppers,** as you would for Paula's Pickled Peppers (p. 79), up to the point where you have removed the stalks and cores, seeds and pith. Now cut up into large squares.

Cook **1½ lb. potatoes** till *just* tender. Drain, cool, peel, cut into large chunks.

Heat **1½ tbs. olive oil** in a heavy pan, fry **2 oz. chopped onion** till translucent. Add the peppers, the potatoes, a pinch of **dry crumbled oregano, 1 tsp. sea-salt.** Add **2-3 tsp. soy sauce,** shake the pan to distribute, turn and blend the potatoes in it, continue frying, with frequent stirring, till potatoes are brown and slightly crisp. (Serves 4)

Accompany with a large salad of thick-sliced ripe **tomatoes** sprinkled with **olive oil, wine vinegar, salt, chopped fresh basil.**

"MUCH TO EAT"

Prepare

1 medium aubergine (about 8 oz.)—peeled, cut in large chunks, salted, put in a sieve under a weight for an hour, then dried and chopped rather fine
1½ oz. mushrooms—sliced thin
4-5 shallots (3 oz.)—sliced in thin rings
1 tbs. fine minced sweet red pepper flesh

1 tbs. fine chopped celery stalk
½ oz. blanched split almonds
4 tomatoes (6 oz.)—peeled, seeded, coarsely chopped
1½ tsp. capers—chopped
¼ tsp. dry crumbled thyme
3 eggs lightly beaten, then mixed with **2 tbs. yoghourt**

Put **2 tbs. olive oil** in a large pan, fry shallot rings gently in it for 3–4 minutes. Add celery, **2–3 crushed garlic cloves,** sweet red pepper. Mix through and fry another 3 minutes till garlic begins to colour. Add the chopped aubergine and sliced mushroom and fry another 5 minutes, stirring frequently. Now the tomatoes, capers, almonds and **1½ tsp. sea-salt.** Stir and cook only 2 minutes longer.

Turn pan contents into a medium size oiled casserole. Pour beaten eggs over, sprinkle with **thyme** and generously with **grated Geska.**

Bake in a moderate oven (350°—Gas 4), covered for the first 25–30 minutes, uncovered for the rest of the time—10–15 minutes more. Let get completely cool. Cut and serve in thick slices, together with Mixed Salad or Antipasto, or plain lettuce salad and Marinated Green Beans. (Serves 6)

MARINATED GREEN BEANS

Slice ½ **lb. young green beans** into diagonal sections, about 1½ inches long.

Heat **1½ tbs. olive oil** in a small pan. Dredge beans lightly with **flour,** turn into the hot oil. Stir and fry till tender but still crisp—about 5 minutes. Add immediately **3 tbs. wine vinegar,** a sprinkling of **sea-salt** and **white pepper.** Serve hot. (3)

PIZZAS

People often say that the French bread they make in France has a quality that is seldom if ever achieved by its imitations abroad. Or, of some other locally produced continental speciality, that "it is good, but not the way it tasted in such-and-such a land". So with pizzas . . . Those we recall having eaten, on a sultry Italian night, as they came hot out of an open air oven, with the oven's glow lighting up the faces of the people waiting round—those pizzas too were quite unique. When taste is wedded to pleasant memory, seemingly taste can never be the same again. Having said all this, the perspicacious reader will wonder—why have a pizza recipe at all? The only answer is—

those who are convinced that pizzas made outside Italy are
not worth considering should kindly go on to the next recipe.
Those willing to try the experiment should carry on. And those
who have never tried pizzas may like to know that they are
discs of leavened dough, topped with things like cheese, tomatoes, onions, herbs, capers, olives and what not—then baked in
the oven. Very simple to prepare, in fact, and very enjoyable to
eat. And here is a simple and almost fool-proof way of making
up the dough:

PIZZA DOUGH (enough for 4 pizzas)

Sift **8 oz. strong plain flour** (see footnote p. 85) into a mixing
bowl, together with **1¼ tsp. sea-salt.** Blend with **1¼ tsp. olive
oil.**

Make up a yeast mixture: Pour **¼ cup warm water** (blood
heat) into a small glass. Add **¼ tsp. demerara sugar** and
¼ tsp. flour. Stir, then sprinkle in **½ tsp. dried baker's yeast.**
Cover the glass, let it stand till mixture is nice and frothy (about
5 minutes).

Have another **¼ cup cold water** ready. When the yeast
mixture has frothed up add it, together with the water, to the
flour. Immediately, with the hands, mix together till a pliable
dough is formed. If necessary, add a *tiny* bit more water.

Knead dough on a lightly floured board for at least 5
minutes. Knead very well, till it is quite elastic. Then oil the
entire surface of the dough lightly with olive oil, put in a polythene bag, close end securely, leave dough to rise for about an
hour at normal kitchen temperature, or longer if in a cold place.

When you are ready to make your pizzas, remove dough from
polythene, punch down and knead again for a few minutes.
Divide into 4 equal portions, form each into a ball. Roll out
balls into thin discs, a little less than ¼ inch thick. Brush surfaces with olive oil. *But before removing dough from polythene, make
up your topping:*

Cottage cheese and onion   Prepare **10 oz. sliced mild onion.**
Fry gently in a little **olive oil** till just softened—don't let it
colour. Cool completely.

Mix **10 oz. cottage cheese** in a bowl together with a little
yoghourt or **cream.** Beat till mixture is light, add **sea-salt** to
taste.

Now remove dough from polythene and make up pizzas. After

brushing pizza surfaces with olive oil, cover each with a layer of onion, and over the onion put a thick layer of cottage cheese. Top the cottage cheese with the remaining onion, arranging it if possible in a lattice-work fashion. Sprinkle over with **dried oregano** and **basil.** Put whole **capers** or **black olive** halves (or both) in the lattice "windows".

Place pizzas on an oiled baking sheet, and baking sheet into a polythene bag. Close end securely. Let pizzas rise for about a ½ hour or till the dough, when pressed lightly, springs back.

Remove from polythene, bake in a hot oven (450°—Gas 8) for 15–20 minutes, or till pizzas are pale biscuit in colour. Serve hot with a Mixed Salad.

Honey and nuts   Made this way, as a sweet, pizzas go perfectly with lots of rich creamy coffee.

After brushing pizza surfaces with **olive oil,** spread over with a generous layer of **mild honey**—warmed slightly first, to make it flow easily—then with **2 oz. almonds and walnuts,** coarsely chopped. Press nuts lightly into dough. Drizzle with more honey, finish with a good sprinkling of **cinnamon** and **sugar.** Place on oiled baking sheet, then in a polythene bag, proceed as before.

COURGETTES (AFTER APICIUS)

Here is a dish, evocative of something—whether it is of ancient Rome must be left to one's own temperament, but the strangeness and beauty of its taste do suggest other times, other climes . . .

Cut ends off **1 lb. courgettes.** Parboil for 5–7 minutes, drain and cool.

Put in a mortar **1 oz. fine chopped walnuts, 1 tsp. minced fennel weed, 2 cloves crushed garlic,** ½ **tsp. dry crumbled oregano,** ½ **tsp. cummin seed, 4 tsp. stoned dates,** minced fine, ½ **tsp. coriander seed.**

Pound everything till well crushed, then add **2 tsp. olive oil** and blend to a paste. Add ½ **cup cold water** in which **2 tsp. sea-salt** has been dissolved.

Cut courgettes into ½ inch thick rounds. Heat **2 tbs. olive oil** in a heavy pan. Fry courgettes lightly till both sides are golden. Pour in the sauce from the mortar, and another ¼ **cup cold water.** Stir gently but thoroughly, so that courgette pieces are well coated. Cover and cook on a continued low heat for 10–12 minutes only—the vegetable should not become too soft.

Serve immediately with dry-cooked rice or plain buttered pasta. (Serves 4)

LASAGNE

Lasagne, as probably everyone knows, are very wide, oblong-shaped pasta. Sometimes they are flat, sometimes they are rippled—but the ripples disappear after they are cooked.

Boil **5 oz. lasagne** in plenty of lightly salted water. Put each oblong in separately, holding it by the edge for a moment if possible, then allowing it to float away before adding the next. This is to prevent them sticking together, and that is the supposed reason why some manufacturers make them with ripples. Boil lasagne till tender, approximately 10–12 minutes. Drain, then place in a bowl of cold water to keep them pliable.

Mix ½ **lb. curd or cottage cheese** with **1 beaten egg** and **1 tbs. soft light-brown sugar.** Add in 1½ **oz. Spanish onion rings** already fried till golden.

Mix ½ **cup yoghourt** with **1 tsp. soft light-brown sugar.** Drain lasagne.

Into the bottom of a pint-and-a-half glass casserole spoon a good layer of the yoghourt. Then as follows:

A single layer of lasagne, then a few spoonfuls of yoghourt spread over. Then another layer of lasagne, followed by one of cheese. Then lasagne, yoghourt, lasagne, cheese till you come to the top, which, hopefully, should be a cheese layer—make it a thick one. Now spoon the rest of the yoghourt over and, if insufficient, make up more yoghourt/sugar mixture—it should cover the top layer of cheese *completely*. Finally, sprinkle over with more soft light-brown sugar.

Bake uncovered, in a moderate oven, for about 30 minutes, or until yoghourt on top has set like a firm custard and the edges are crisp and brown. Serve hot. (Serves 3–4)

As a complete meal, start with Antipasto, then go on to Lasagne with a plain lettuce salad and a sweet white wine.

GESKA CHEESE MARBLES

Prepare a mixture of the following

1 cup grated Geska cheese
½ **cup bread-crumbs, untoasted**
¼ **tsp. dry crumbled basil**
2 chopped spring onions or wild garlic stems
1½ **tsp. sea-salt**
2 beaten eggs

Mix together thoroughly, then form into large marbles. Break another **egg** into a bowl and beat.

Dip marbles into egg, then in plain flour—and repeat the process once again. Fry in deep hot oil till golden. Drain, serve hot on cocktail sticks. (Makes about 24)

> Does not nature produce enough simple vegetable foods to satisfy? And if not content with such simplicity can you not, by the mixture of them, produce infinite variations?
>
> LEONARDO DA VINCI

Spain and Portugal

There exists a mysterious herb which has
the power of restoring sight but, alas, only
the swallows know where it grows . . .

Old Spanish Legend

And since the swallows continue to guard the secret well, no
one has yet discovered the unknown dwelling place of the
miraculous herb. But other herbs, also once alien and unknown,
have found their way to Spain and Portugal, and brought with
them a touch of the legendary. For the successive waves of
invasion and infiltration from the east opened up the land to
new and "exotic" crops—the flourishing vine and olive which
now luxuriate over the Andalusian plain, and which the Greeks
introduced, the rice and sugar cane which the Arabs planted.
Pomegranate took root, fig trees blossomed . . . The orient and
occident intertwined.

Even though more than 400 years have gone since the Moors
were expelled, the old ways of preparing food still remain. And
subtly woven with the native cookery are flamboyant traces of
clove, cinnamon and nutmeg, chilli pepper, caraway and
sesame, cummin, saffron and mint—aromatic essences in which
ancient memories of the Caliphates still survive.

PISTO

A beautifully mellow and rich tasting ragout of Mediterranean
vegetables, with a touch of hot chilli:

cut **4 oz. courgettes** into ¼-inch rounds
and **1 small sweet green pepper (4 oz.)** into ¼-inch wide
  strips
slice **3 tomatoes (8 oz.)** into eighths
dice **3 oz. sweet Spanish onion**
remove seeds from **1 dry red chilli pepper** and crumble

Heat **2 tbs. olive oil** in a heavy pan. Fry onion slowly till
creamy in colour (4–5 minutes). Add **a crushed clove of garlic** and cook gently, another 2 minutes. Now add the green

pepper strips, cover the pan, continue cooking gently, 8 minutes more. Now strew in the tomatoes and courgettes and this seasoning: **1 tsp. sea-salt** (or more if desired), $\frac{1}{4}$ **tsp. dry crumbled mint,** the crumbled chilli pepper, a light sprinkling of **demerara sugar.** Cover the pan and cook slowly, 25–30 minutes. Serve hot over **dry-cooked rice** or with **Sesame Potatoes** (p. 129). (Serves 2)

BREAD SALAD

A most refreshing summer luncheon appetizer.

For each portion prepare the following:

an inch-thick slice of day-old bread with crust removed, then cut into small cubes
1 small tomato—chopped fine
2 tbs. very fine minced celery
1 tbs. chopped parsley
1 tsp. fine chopped sweet red pepper
$\frac{1}{2}$ **tsp. sea-salt**
4 black olives—stoned and cut small
a pinch of dry crumbled basil
a pinch of fresh ground black pepper

Put bread cubes into a glass salad bowl, soak with **2–3 tsp. lemon juice** and one of **wine vinegar,** plus **2 tbs. olive oil.** Soak about 10 minutes. Then add the vegetable ingredients and seasoning, mix and mash well with a fork.

Try it when appetites are feeble or waning—see how quickly they revive.

MUSHROOM SPREAD

Prepare

4 oz. button mushrooms—cleaned and sliced fine
$\frac{1}{2}$ **oz. walnuts**—pulverized in the electric grinder
a generous $\frac{1}{2}$ **tsp. of chopped sweet red pepper**
a small onion (1 oz.)—chopped very fine

Fry onion till softened and lightly coloured in **1 tbs. olive oil.** Add mushrooms, ground walnuts, red pepper, a scant $\frac{3}{4}$ **tsp. sea-salt, 1 tsp. sherry.** Fry gently, 7–8 minutes, stir frequently. Remove pan contents to a wooden board, scrape out anything that remains in the pan, then chop till you have a creamy purée, adding a pinch of **chilli powder** on the way. Chill. Serve on **melba toast** or **crackers.**

Many of the traditions that linger longest with people are those concerned with food. When all else is in danger of being forgotten, memories of tastes and smells experienced in childhood can still haunt us. We can think of Proust and his *madeleines*, for example, although he remembered a lot else besides. Here is a dish which Spanish Jews remember:

MERENJENA PRETA ALA SPAÑOLA

. . . Which, in *Ladino*,* simply means "black tomatoes in the Spanish style".

Wash **2 medium aubergines (12 oz.)**, leave peel on. Cut into ½ **inch thick slices,** lengthways. Salt generously, put in a sieve under a weight for an hour, rinse and pat dry.

Cut **7–8 good sized shallots** into thin slices. Heat **1½ tbs. olive oil,** slowly, in a large heavy pan. Arrange the shallot slices in a single layer in the pan. If the pan bottom isn't covered, add more shallot slices. Place a layer of aubergine slices on top. Arrange on each a wafer thin slice of **lemon,** rind included, and **2 or 3 strips of sweet red pepper.** Follow with the rest of the aubergine slices, similarly decorated. Drizzle over with olive oil, add slowly ½ **cup water.** Cover pan, cook gently for 15 minutes.

Meanwhile, in a small saucepan, bring to the boil: ½ **cup water, ¼ cup demerara sugar, 5 tbs. cider vinegar, 1 tbs. seedless raisins, 1 tbs. butter, ½ tsp. sea-salt, 1 crushed garlic clove.** Simmer 10–12 minutes.

Pour sweet-sour sauce, very slowly, over aubergine slices, re-cover pan, continue cooking gently for another 45–6c minutes, till vegetable is tender without falling apart.

Remove pan from heat and let cool a little. Then, with a spatula, transfer aubergine slices carefully to a large shallow platter. Each piece should retain its red pepper/lemon decoration.

Reduce remaining sauce in pan over a brisk heat for 5 minutes, or till slightly thickened. Spoon over the aubergine slices. Let cool completely before serving with Saffron Rice. (Serves 5)

SAFFRON RICE

Cook **1 cup rice** as for dry-cooked rice (p. 89), but with a

* A language based on Old Castilian and still used by many Jews whose ancestors came from Spain.

pinch of **saffron** added to the water. Let cool completely, then add: **1 tbs. olive oil, sea-salt** to taste, **2 tsp. minced spring onion, 1½ tbs. toasted pine kernels, 2 tsp. fine chopped sweet red pepper,** a squeeze of **lemon juice.** Mix through well.

SWEET POTATO MASH

And here is a dish which recalls the taste, and the texture, of roasted chestnuts:

Peel ¾ **lb. sweet potato** and cut into small pieces. Steam or boil in very little water till tender. Drain, mash to a purée. Add ⅛ **tsp. cayenne pepper,** a pinch of **nutmeg, 1 tbs. butter, 1 tbs. cream, 1 tsp. sea-salt.** Whip through thoroughly and serve hot. (Serves 3)

CHICK PEA SCRAMBLE

Chick peas, *garbanzos* in Spain, are another of those versatile denizens of the edible world. They went to ancient wars in soldiers' knapsacks, they were celebrated in peace at harvest rites. Sustaining, nourishing and tasty—either in their original shape, or transformed by man's insatiable need for variety— they have earned their place in the Mediterranean diet.

When Columbus demonstrated how an egg could be stood on its end, he fascinated not only contemporary Spaniards but generations of schoolboys to come. The egg is another thing Spaniards hold highly and, with chick peas and olives, it makes a delightful mélange.

For 2 portions do as follows: put **2 oz. dried chick peas** in water to cover. Add a pinch of **bicarbonate of soda.** Rinse in fresh water the next day, put to boil till completely tender.* Drain, keep aside.

In a heavy pan, fry **1 oz. diced sweet onion** and **6 stoned black olives,** cut in halves. Fry till onion is creamy in colour, then add the drained chick peas. Fry and stir another 5 minutes, then pour over **4 well beaten eggs,** seasoned with **salt, black pepper** and a spoonful of **cream.** Proceed as for scrambled eggs. When done, sprinkle generously with **chopped parsley,** serve with a green salad, bread and butter, white wine. (Serves 3)

* You can get tinned, ready-cooked chick peas from America, labelled appropriately "Garbanzos". Obtainable at good provision stores.

SPICY CHICK PEA PUFFS

Mix together

4 oz. chick pea flour (available in Spanish provis
as *garbanzo* flour)
2 eggs
½ tsp. cummin seed
½ tsp. coriander powder
¼ tsp. chilli powder
1 large garlic clove—crushed
2½-3 tbs. water
1 tsp. sea-salt

Make up a batter that will fall easily from the end of a spoon.
Drop by spoonfuls into deep hot oil, fry till rich golden. Drain,
serve. Enough for 3–4. (Excellent as cocktail snacks, or with
Layered Salad.)

LAYERED SALAD

A very colourful and tempting salad, practically a meal on its
own. Serve in individual glass bowls to make the most of its
variety.

Arrange layers as follows:

thick slices of large tomatoes, sprinkled over with **fresh
chopped basil** and **olive oil**
artichoke hearts (tinned) spooned over with **mild salad
dressing**
cold cooked potato slices, decorated with **chopped
capers, chopped black olives, toasted crushed
almonds,** and a swirl of **mayonnaise**
tender **watercress leaves,** stalks discarded, sprinkled with
tarragon vinegar
over the top—criss-cross strips of **red pimento**

Accompany with generous chunks of crusty bread.

LEEK PAELLA

Many dishes that are usually served hot can often be eaten cold,
and it is surprising how many times they do taste better when
they're cold. Into this category comes our Leek Paella, a very
modest but flavoursome dish that can be eaten either way.

Trim stalks and leaves of ¼ **lb. young leeks.** Discard any
tough or withered green parts. Wash very carefully, making
sure to remove any sand or grit between the leaves. Cut in
inch-long sections.

Heat 2½ tbs. olive oil in a large frying pan and add the leeks. Fork through to break open the layers. Cook gently for 5 minutes, stir occasionally. Then add 1 cup patna rice, well washed. Raise heat, mix through and fry, stirring and frying till rice is lightly flecked with gold. Now add: 3 tomatoes peeled, cored, seeded and coarsely chopped, 1 tsp. demerara sugar, 1½ tsp. sea-salt, a little black pepper, 1¼ cups boiling water. Cover pan and cook gently till liquid is absorbed and rice is tender. Add a tiny bit more water only if necessary. Cool entirely. Sprinkle over with a generous squeeze of lemon juice. (3-4)

FIVE-VEGETABLE PAELLA

A more decorative paella, decorative to the eye, to the palate— reserve for more decorative occasions. Serve hot.

Prepare

> 2 oz. fine chopped sweet onion
> 3 large tomatoes—skinned, seeded, coarsely chopped
> 1¾ cups rich soup stock (from Instant Soup Mix) and
> additionally coloured with a pinch of saffron
> ¼ cup young green beans—parboiled, then cut into
> diagonal sections
> 2 oz. sweet red pepper—finely chopped
> 1 small carrot—coarsely grated

Have ready

> ¾ cup fresh young green peas

Heat 2-3 tbs. olive oil in a large heavy pan. Fry the onions slowly for 3 minutes. Add 2 crushed garlic cloves, fry 2 minutes longer. Now: 1¼ cups washed patna rice and raise heat to medium. Fry and stir till rice is lightly flecked with gold. Then add the tomatoes and the soup stock, bring to the boil, cover, simmer 10 minutes. Add finally the parboiled green beans, the young green peas, the grated carrot, the sweet red pepper. Season with sea-salt and a sprinkle of black pepper. Re-cover the pan, continue simmering gently till liquid absorbs and rice is tender. Again, as before, add a little more liquid only if necessary. Steam, covered, for about 15 minutes at the side of the cooker. Serve piled on a long heated platter, top with toasted pine kernels and split spring onions. (4-5)

GASPACHO

A long time ago, Spain and Portugal were considered one country, their inhabitants one people. The land was Iberia to the Greeks, Hispania to the Romans and latterly, to most others, the Peninsula. Today, though divided by language and frontier, there are still many similarities in food preparation. Our Gaspacho, for example, is a Portuguese variant on a Spanish concoction, very popular as an afternoon snack with a glass of wine in the province of Alentejo.

Slice a good **white bread** into thick slices. Sprinkle each generously with **olive oil,** then cover half of them with **tomato slices, cucumber slices, onion slices, chopped black olives,** a little **minced garlic,** some chopped fresh herbs like **basil, parsley, coriander,** and, finally, some **sea-salt.** Cap with the remaining bread slices and drizzle over with more olive oil. Arrange the *Gaspacho* on a large plate, cover over with another plate equal in size, weight the top so that the contents are well pressed down. Chill a few hours. But if you're in a hurry, remove *Gaspacho* sooner from refrigerator, raise bread caps carefully, strew small cubes of ice or crushed ice over the vegetables, replace caps, serve 5 minutes later—to give the ice a chance to melt.

AÇORDA

A typical country soup from Portugal. Simple, almost fundamental in its ingredients, it turns out with a surprisingly strange and agreeable flavour. An excellent antidote to too much rich living . . . ?

Into $1\frac{1}{2}$ **pints boiling water** break up $\frac{1}{2}$ **lb. bread**—preferably rye or wholemeal—with crust removed. Reduce heat to a simmer, then add: **2 cloves garlic** sliced in halves, **2 tsp. sea-salt,** a sprinkling of **black pepper.** Simmer till bread is almost a mush, then spoon it, together with the cooked garlic, into a sieve. Press through thoroughly, then return to the saucepan. Reheat well, stirring constantly, serve in thick earthenware bowls. Sprinkle surfaces with **chopped parsley** and **spring onion.** (Serves 4–5)

CALDO VERDE

Another country soup, not so thick as Açorda, but thick enough.

Peel $1\frac{1}{4}$ **lb. potatoes.** Rinse and shake dry **half a small green cabbage.** Chop both fairly fine.

Heat **2 tbs. olive oil** in a large saucepan, sauté ½ **large sweet onion,** cut into rings, till pale golden, then add the potato and cabbage, fry and stir a further 5 minutes. Pour in **2 pints freshly boiled water,** simmer till soup has thickened. Season with **salt** and fresh ground **black pepper.** (4–5)

PORTUGUESE SALADS

I. Wash a small head of **crisp lettuce,** shake leaves dry, shred coarsely. Place in a large salad bowl. Add: ¼ **cup very young green beans,** cut in narrow diagonal sections, ¼ **cup small, tender sugar peas, 2 spring onions,** cut in lengthwise strips, **2 tomatoes,** cut in eighths. (Enough for 4)

Put in a mortar ½ **tsp. demerara sugar, 1 tsp. sea-salt,** a fair sliver of **garlic, 4–5 fresh mint leaves,** medium in size. Grind to a smooth paste, then add **2 tsp. lemon juice** and combine everything thoroughly, then **4 tbs. olive oil** in a thin steady stream—stir briskly. Finally, **2 tsp. cream,** little by little, and amalgamating it well before adding more. Pour over and blend through the salad.

Serve with bread fingers fried till crisp in olive oil, then drained and salted.

II. Pile crisp **lettuce leaves** into individual salad bowls. Strew over with a few **sweet onion rings,** some bland **black stoned olives, 1 tsp. capers.**

Dressing: Put into a bottle **4 tbs. sweet purple grape juice, 4 tbs. olive oil, 4 tsp. wine vinegar,** ½ **tsp. sea-salt,** a large bruised **mint leaf.** Cap bottle, shake vigorously to emulsify, chill well for 15 minutes. (Enough for 4)

GARLIC BREAD

"Better a slice of bread and garlic eaten at one's own table than a hundred dishes under a stranger's roof." So goes a Spanish proverb, seemingly modest about life's pleasures, seemingly scorning them in its pride. Yet who, after all, expects to be invited into strangers' homes with banquets set with a hundred dishes—who but a dreamer, perhaps? And if that slice of bread and garlic means something else—*Garlic Bread*, for instance—then the pleasure is less than modest, it is more like shrewd. For what is more exhilarating than a slice of garlic bread and a glass of young red wine?

Note: If you are not entirely convinced by this "Spanish" reasoning, you may at least like to know that our garlic bread is going to be grilled, and the garlic essences transformed into something eloquent and mild . . .

In a mortar grind together **1 fresh mint leaf, 1 dry red chilli pepper,** seeds removed, **¾ tsp. sea-salt, 1 crushed garlic clove.** Blend till creamy, then add **1½ tsp. lemon juice** (half a small lemon), stir in well, then, very slowly, **2 tbs. olive oil** and amalgamate. (Enough to coat 4–6 bread slices.)

Toast thick slices of white or rye bread on one side. Remove from grill, spread untoasted sides with liquid mixture. Return to grill and grill till sizzling and brown at the edges. Serve immediately (with young red wine).

AUBERGINE OILBAKE

Make deep, lengthwise incisions in **4 small aubergines (about 3 oz. each)**—cut in about half-way. Spread cut edges open slightly, dredge in with salt, let stand for an hour. Rinse out and dry. Scoop out a little of the aubergine flesh.

In a mortar, grind **1–2 dry red chilli peppers** with seeds removed, together with **1 tsp. sea-salt.** Then add **2 oz. fine minced onion, 1 large crushed clove of garlic, 2 tbs. untoasted bread-crumbs.** Pound to a fairly smooth paste, blend with **1 tbs. fine chopped green coriander** or **2 tsp. fresh parsley.** Force this mixture into the cut aubergines, press edges back together.

Arrange aubergines in a small heavy pan. Pour over with **½ cup olive oil.** Bring to a light boil, reduce to a gentle simmer, cover pan. Turn aubergines from time to time, carefully, till tender and evenly cooked (about 35 minutes). Serve hot. (Serves 3–4)

LITTLE CAULIFLOWER FRITTERS

Wash **1 small cauliflower** and separate flowerets. Steam till just tender, then mince fine. Add to **4 well beaten eggs.** Blend with **3 tbs. flour, 2 tbs. fine minced onion, 1 tsp. sea-salt, ¼ tsp. cayenne pepper, ¼ tsp. dry crumbled thyme.**

Drop by spoonfuls into deep hot oil, cook till golden and puffed. Drain on absorbent paper, serve hot with Chilled Stuffed Tomatoes. (Serves 5–6)

CHILLED STUFFED TOMATOES

For *each* serving prepare **2 medium sized tomatoes (about 4 oz.).**

tops off tomatoes, scoop out pulp and seeds and
h

oiled egg yolk—mashed
unded tsp. capers—minced very fine
f crushed garlic
a-salt
i fresh mint leaf—chopped
8 tsp. bread-crumbs (untoasted)
a sprinkle of black pepper

Mix all ingredients as smoothly as possible, pile into the
tomato shells high and generously. Top each with a **walnut
half,** wrap individually in foil. Chill for 1–2 hours. Serve on
crisp **lettuce leaves.**

GREEN-RED EGGS

After blanching in freshly boiled water, skin **4 tomatoes
(8 oz.)**, core, chop small. Heat **1½ tbs. olive oil** in a large pan,
add **2 crushed cloves of garlic,** stir and fry gently till
beginning to colour. Then add the tomatoes, together with
½ **tsp. coriander powder,** ½ **tsp. sea-salt,** a sprinkle of
demerara sugar. Simmer till slightly thickened—about 10
minutes—then add **2 tsp. lemon juice.**

Meanwhile, slice **1 very small sweet green pepper (2 oz.)**
into thin strips. Put strips under the grill and heat till skin is
crackling and golden-blistered, turn over, then grill till
slightly shrivelled. Remove from grill, arrange over the tomato.

Now beat **3 eggs** till frothy, season with ½ **tsp. sea-salt**
and a little **black pepper,** pour over the tomato and green
pepper. Cover the pan, cook till eggs are just setting, divide in
half, serve on hot plates. (Serves 2)

POMEGRANATES

The juicy pomegranate, a symbol of beauty to many cultures,
appears on ancient Spanish vase paintings. In a land which
reports of some of its regions, ironically, as having nine months
of winter and *three months of hell*, the pomegranate is under-
standably appreciated.

Pomegranates should be bought when their skins have a rosy
blush to them. They should then be cut in half and served in
glass bowls surrounded by crushed ice—together with spoons
for scooping out the liquid encased seeds. The pips should not
be eaten.

For a cooling summer drink, scoop out the seeds from **4 ripe pomegranates,** put in a muslin bag. Twist the bag over a bowl until all the liquid possible has been squeezed out. Stir in fine **castor sugar** to taste, chill thoroughly. Serve in glasses decorated with a sprig of **mint.**

MOORISH RICE CREAM

Make up ¼ **cup powdered rice** by grinding plain rice in the electric grinder.

Bring to the boil a solution of ½ **cup water, 1 pint milk.** Reduce heat. Stir powdered rice in very slowly. Continue stirring till the mixture thickens (about 7 minutes). Then add **5 tbs. demerara sugar** and continue stirring, and simmering, till the liquid begins to coat the spoon (about another 12–15 minutes). Now add **1 tsp. rosewater,** ½ **tsp. grated lemon rind,** a good pinch of **nutmeg.** Simmer another 2 minutes, pour into individual glass bowls. Decorate with **chopped nuts.** Chill. (Serves 4)

France

There is a general responsibility of humanity that binds us not only to the animals, who have life and feeling, but even to trees and plants. We owe equity to men and kindness and benevolence to all other creatures.

MONTAIGNE

GASCON SAUCE

Gascons are usually noted for things other than sauces, although sauce, in its slangier meaning of "cheek" or "lip", is a uniquely Gascon attribute.

Here is a sauce, provocative of nothing more than an ingratiating wish to blend with other friendly foods, a Gascon sauce with modest manners.

Stone **4 oz. black olives** and mince into a mortar. Pound till relatively smooth, add **2 tsp. grated Geska cheese** and amalgamate. Then **2 tbs. olive oil,** little by little, until the whole begins to thicken nicely. Then **1 tbs. lemon juice** and mix in well.

Serve over **boiled new potatoes** or **hard-boiled eggs.** Or as a noodle dressing—but heat it gently first (enough for 4). Or as a filling for Basque Omelette.

BASQUE OMELETTE

Make your **3 egg omelette(s)** in the usual way. When about half done, and the top is still runny, add 2-3tbs. of any of the following fillings:

(1) *Gascon Sauce* (see above)

(2) *Plain tomato and basil sauce:* Blanch and peel **4 tomatoes (8 oz.),** core, chop small. Simmer in **1½ tbs. olive oil,** together with a generous sprinkling of **basil**—fresh or dried—**½ tsp. sea-salt,** a light sprinkle **demerara sugar.** Simmer till lightly thickened (10–12 minutes), add **2 tsp. lemon juice** and stir through. (Enough for 3–4 omelettes)

(3) *Grilled red peppers:* Cut the flesh of **1 medium size
sweet red pepper (4 oz.)** into thin strips. Grill under a medium heat till blistered and slightly shrivelled—grill both sides.
(Enough for 4 omelettes)

Let the filling cook with the eggs until the omelette is done,
fold over, slide out on to a heated platter.

Serve with Salade Benvenuto.

SALADE BENVENUTO

The rather pretentious sounding title of this plain lettuce salad
should not put you off. Its origin, obscure like many other fancy
culinary names, is probably derived from the following.

When Benvenuto Cellini was imprisoned, a not infrequent
experience in his turbulent younger days, he happened to be
served with some greens which, as he chewed them, gritted
unpleasantly through his teeth. He realized immediately that
one of his enemies had bribed the prison cook to include a
small amount of crushed diamond in the dish—a rather
hideous way of doing someone in. But thanks to the cupidity
of men, not only of prison cooks, the diamond had been
substituted with glass, or something equally worthless—a
fact which solaced Benvenuto, and the history of western art
as well.

Nowadays, when we eat lettuce and it grits through our
teeth, we can be reasonably sure that the cause is only sand.
With or without sand, however, a plain lettuce salad frequently
turns out to be one of the most disappointing of salads. Often
served limp, and with an insipid dressing, the texture and
delicate flavour are barely discernible.

To make a salad the way Benvenuto would have liked it—
and this is probably the point of the title—do as follows:

Wash a **firm head of lettuce,** leaf by leaf, removing any of
the wilted edges or leaves. Shake lightly, but dry as possible,
put in a covered container into the refrigerator for at least 2
hours. When you take it out again the leaves should be tight and
crisp and bouncy-looking, almost as though they were fresh
picked.

For a medium size head of round lettuce prepare the following dressing: Pulverize in a mortar ¼ **tsp. dry basil** or **dill** (or a
¼ tsp. combination of both), together with ¼ **tsp. sea-salt.**
Pulverize till a beautiful green powder results—the finer the
powder, the smoother your dressing. Add a sliver of **garlic** and

continue the process.* Now add **1 tbs. olive oil,** bit by bit, till it is well amalgamated. Then ⅛ **tsp. mild honey.** Finally, ½ **tsp. lemon juice** and a dash of **wine vinegar**—which will bind everything into a creamy whole.

Immediately before serving, tear the lettuce leaves in smallish pieces into a salad bowl. Give the dressing a final spin in the mortar and pour in. Lightly toss the lettuce over and over till each piece beams with a thin coating of dressing.

POTATO AND POIS MANGE TOUT SALAD

The young peas called *pois mange tout* are usually available during the spring months. They are a delicate variety of green pea which can be eaten whole, pod and all.

Blanch ¼ **lb. mange tout** for 1 minute, drain, cool, cut into quarters.

Boil 1½ **lb. waxy potatoes** until tender but still firm. Cool, peel, cut into ½ inch slices. Then place in a salad bowl together with 1½ **tbs. chopped sweet green pepper, 7-8 sliced radishes, 1 tbs. chopped spring onion, 2 tbs. toasted crushed almonds,** and the mange tout quarters.

Make up a dressing: **4 tbs. good salad cream, 3 tbs. olive oil, 4 tsp. wine vinegar, 1 tsp. sea-salt, ½ tsp. dry crumbled basil.** Blend well, pour over the ingredients in the salad bowl, amalgamate carefully, serve. (4)

An excellent salad for taking on picnics as well. It needs only the addition of French bread and butter, chunks of cheese, wine and some fruit to make a delightfully simple alfresco meal.

FENNEL BUTTER

Chop **1 tbs. fresh fennel weed** exceedingly fine, add to **4 tbs. slightly softened butter.** Sprinkle over with **1 tsp. sea-salt** and work everything together till perfectly blended. Then put aside in a cool place or refrigerate till needed.

Especially good on boiled potatoes, string beans, young carrots, young green peas. Just drop in small gobs on the hot vegetables, shake well so that the butter melts and the fresh green fennel flavour is absorbed. Serve immediately.

---

* A *chapon* can be used by those who dread the suggestion of raw garlic, yet still want to savour the admirable taste it imparts to a salad. Rub a hard crust of bread with a cut clove of garlic and toss through the lettuce when the dressing is put in. It will give the faintest hint of garlic flavour without calling attention to itself.

PAIN PERDU QUÉBECOIS

This rather more elaborate form of *pain perdu* is a favourite with French-Canadians and one of the pleasantest weekend breakfasts imaginable.

Slice good quality **white bread** into ½-inch slices (**6–8 slices**).

Cut razor-thin slices of **lemon** and **orange,** leaving the peel on. Divide into quarters. Put in a small plate, immerse in good liqueur like **Cointreau** or **Grand Marnier.**

Break **2 eggs** into a bowl, add 2–3 tbs. **cream.** Beat well. Have a heavy frying pan heating with **2 tbs. olive oil.** Dip each bread slice quickly but thoroughly into the egg mixture, place in the pan. Fry till golden brown on both sides, drain on crumpled brown paper. Add more oil from time to time as necessary.

Put the crisp fried bread on to hot plates, decorate each slice with plenty of the liqueur soaked orange and lemon quarters (and whatever liqueur remains), drench the whole with **maple syrup.** Serve with large steaming cups of milky coffee. (3)

MAIZE GALETTES

In the Bordelais, maize, which has been cultivated for centuries, still forms the basis of many of the region's dishes. One of the most agreeable of these is the *galette*, or little cake.

To ½ **cup maize meal*** add **1 well-beaten egg, 3 tbs. soft light-brown sugar** (lightly packed), a scant ½ **tsp. grated orange rind, ⅛ tsp. cinnamon, 1 tbs. brandy** (optional), a small amount of **cold water—approximately 2 tbs.**—and blend well. The mixture should be very light but not runny, almost like a thick cake batter.

Heat **1 tbs. butter** and **3 tbs. olive oil** in a large heavy pan. Bring to medium heat. Drop *galette* mixture into the pan by spoonfuls, spread each out lightly with the back of the spoon. Fry till brown on both sides. Drain. Dust immediately with a mixture of **powdered sugar** and **cinnamon.** (8–10 *galettes*)

Try sipping a good white wine and nibbling these *galettes*— a very tasty combination it is.

* The brand styled "3 Minute Yellow Corn Meal" is one of the best, available at good provision stores.

WOODLAND CASSEROLE

Prepare

6 oz. drained (tinned) chestnuts—break up coarsely
1 leek (3 oz.)—wash well, cut into thin rounds, then separate into rings
2–3 stalks of wild garlic (optional)—chop coarsely
6 oz. mushrooms—cut in ¼-inch thick slices

Heat **5 tsp. olive oil** in a 2 pint earthenware casserole. Fry leek-rings gently for 7 minutes. Add chopped wild garlic—or **2 crushed cloves ordinary garlic**—fry a few minutes longer. Add the mushrooms. Fry 5 minutes more. Then the chestnuts together with **1 tsp. sea-salt.** Stir through, cook 2–3 minutes, level surface off lightly, remove from heat.

Make up a batter: **3 oz. maize meal, 2 eggs, 1 tsp. sea-salt, ¼ cup buttermilk, 1 tsp. olive oil, ½ tsp. bicarbonate of soda.** Blend well, pour over the ingredients in the casserole. Bake uncovered (at 400°—Gas 6) for ½ hour, or till the top is firm and richly golden. (4–5)

GRILLED OLIVE BREAD

An excellent party snack, an appetite awakener, or an enjoyable light supper on its own. The long fresh loaves of French bread are best for its preparation but not essential.

Stone **¼ lb. firm black olives** and mince into a mortar. Add **a small crushed clove of garlic, 1½ tbs. minced capers, 1 tsp. sea-salt** (less, if your olives are particularly briny-tasting already). Pound and mix to a relatively smooth paste, add **3–4 tbs. olive oil,** bit by bit, until the whole becomes the consistency of a fairly thin spread.

Cut **French bread** into 4-inch lengths and slice each length in half. Spread the cut surface of each piece generously with the olive mixture, toast under the grill till fragrant and sizzling.

If you are using ordinary white or rye bread, cut into thick slices, toast one side of each, spread the olive mixture on the untoasted side, grill it. (7–8 slices of olive bread)

Variation: Top each piece of olive bread with **a thin slice of tomato,** then grill.
Serve with Salade Niçoise.

SALADE NIÇOISE

Use a **lettuce** with a crisp firm heart. Cut into quarters or eighths, arrange at the bottom of individual salad bowls.

Over each lettuce portion distribute the following: **stoned black and green olives, the yolks of hard-boiled eggs,** cut in halves, **chopped spring onions, thin-sliced radishes,** firm but ripe **tomato slices,** thick cut **cucumber slices,** peeled and seeded. Flavour with **olive oil, wine vinegar, grated Geska cheese, sea-salt,** fresh or dry **basil leaves** (chopped or crumbled).

GREEN AIOLI

Aioli, the "butter" of southern France, is an intoxicating kind of mayonnaise which can be used to enchant the taste of any vegetable, raw or cooked. The form of it given here, green *aioli,* is a variation with a distinctness of its own. Though the amount of garlic called for may seem alarming, the mellowing qualities of olive oil and fresh green herb transform it into a subtly tingling delight.

In a mortar crush almost to a liquid state **4–5 medium size leaves of fresh basil.** Then pound together with **4 crushed cloves of garlic** and ½ **tsp. sea-salt.** Add the **yolk of a small fresh egg** and amalgamate well. The next part is a little tedious but necessary—⅓ **cup best quality olive oil** is added, *drop by drop* at first, and stirred in briskly. Patience . . . it will not be long before you are rewarded by the sight of the mixture turning into a homogeneous mass. When this happens you will notice that about half the olive oil has been used up, and now you can add it in as a thin steady stream, but still stirring briskly so that it is constantly being absorbed. When the *aioli* is done it should have the consistency of fresh churned butter, in this case a glistening pale-green butter. Pile it into a small pottery bowl and surround it with a variety of vegetables **—boiled new potatoes, thick slices of tomato and cucumber, baby carrots, young boiled beets, raw cauliflower.** It is also perfect as a filling for avocados, slightly thinned down with yoghourt.

Variation: When fresh herbs are unobtainable, substitute with dry—scant ½ **tsp. basil** (or **dill**), pulverized to a smooth green powder together with the sea-salt before the garlic is added.

AUBERGINES BÉARNAISE

Choose **aubergines** of the slender variety—**2 medium or 3 small sized (10 oz.).** Wash, cut into ¾-inch slices crosswise, leave skin on. Put in a large sieve or strainer, sprinkle each layer with **sea-salt,** sprinkle well, place a weight on top, leave for an hour. Then pat dry on a tea towel or absorbent paper.

Cut **15-20 purple grapes** into halves and remove seeds. Gently heat **5-6 tbs. olive oil** in a large heavy pan. Add **1½ oz. sweet onion rings, 1 tsp. crushed coriander seed,** let cook slowly 4-5 minutes. Now arrange in the aubergine slices, overlapping if necessary. Cover and cook for 10 minutes. Turn slices over, cover, cook a further 5 minutes. Add **a large crushed clove of garlic,** together with **4 whole cloves,** cover, cook 4-5 minutes longer. Now turn the slices once again, carefully, and add the purple grape halves. Cover, cook 4-5 minutes. Pour in ¾ **wineglass dry red wine,** shake the pan lightly to distribute, cover, cook to completion—another 10-15 minutes approximately. About 5 minutes before removing from heat, sprinkle in **1 tbs. demerara sugar.**

When the mixture has cooled somewhat, spoon it carefully into a small deep bowl—see that the aubergine slices remain whole if possible. Let cool completely before serving. It's even better if left in the refrigerator and eaten the following day. (Serves 3-4)

The tedium of following this recipe is made up for by the result. Béarnaise aubergines are wonderfully aromatic, and the unusual flavour is redolent of wine, grapes, oil and spices. There is no other dish which tastes quite like it, except, perhaps . . .

COURGETTES BÉARNAISE

And these are made in precisely the same way as above—with **10 oz. courgettes** cut into ⅓-inch slices—only it is usual to vary the pattern of red wine and grapes with white. But there is absolutely nothing against your using the red if you wish.

And when there's no wine in the house, and someone has eaten the grapes you were saving for your Béarnaise, do not despair. Proceed in the same way without the wine, and for the grapes substitute **seedless raisins** which have been properly plumped in fresh-boiled water for 10 minutes.

DÉLICE DE CHAMPIGNONS

Clean **6 oz. firm button mushrooms**—only those with the closed caps will do. Cut into large chunks. Set aside.

Heat **3-4 tbs. olive oil** in a heavy pan, add about **20 lightly crushed coriander seeds,** cook slowly for 2 minutes. Now add the mushroom chunks and cook a further 2 minutes. Now add the following: **15 seedless green grapes,** cut in halves, the **juice of a medium size orange,** a fragment of **bay-leaf,** a small crushed **garlic clove, 3–4 tbs. medium-sweet white wine,** a pinch of **sea-salt, 1 tsp. demerara sugar** and, finally, a squeeze of **lemon juice.**

Continue cooking gently—another 4–5 minutes at most— then transfer mushrooms and grapes to a warm bowl. Leave pan on the heat, reduce sauce by simmering a further 4–5 minutes, pour over the mushrooms and grapes.

Serve hot over a bed of **dry-cooked rice** to which has been added a suggestion of **grated lemon rind.**

Serve cold as an hors d'oeuvre accompanied with bread and butter and glasses of chilled white wine. (2–3)

PRUNES AND POTATOES

Albert Schweitzer, who was born in Alsace, and spent an idyllic childhood there, speaks in his autobiography of the abundance of its fruitful orchards. The plums (and prunes) of Alsace appear in varying guises throughout the year—in tartlets, puddings and soups during the summer, in preserves and in filling casseroles in wintertime. The recipe below is for a popular country dish, satisfying even to the heartiest of appetites, and attractive to look at when the juices of the prunes have stained the potatoes a rich deep brown:

Heat **1½–2 tbs. olive oil** in a large heavy pan. Add ½ **Spanish onion,** coarsely chopped, fry till light brown. Now add: **1¼ lb. peeled potatoes,** cut in large chunks, ½ **lb. washed prunes, 1 tsp. lightly crushed coriander seed, 2–3 crushed cloves of garlic.** Stir and fry vigorously for 2 minutes, add just enough cold water to immerse the ingredients, reduce heat, cover pan. Let cook gently for 30 minutes. Then season with **1 rounded tsp. sea-salt, 1 tbs. soy sauce, ½ tsp. soft light-brown sugar, 1 tbs. mild honey.** Blend well, cover pan, continue cooking slowly, allowing steam to escape. After 30 minutes more, turn potatoes over carefully and continue cooking—covered—until they are well glazed and brown. (Enough for 4)

Serve with Sweet-Sour Cabbage Salad.

SWEET-SOUR CABBAGE SALAD

Wash and drain **12 oz. Savoy cabbage leaves,** remove tough ribs, shred thin. Blanch in freshly boiled water for 1 minute, drain and cool.

Combine with this dressing: **2 tbs. olive oil, 1 tsp. sea-salt,** a pinch of **dry crumbled oregano, 2 tsp. demerara sugar, 1 tbs. wine vinegar,** ¼ tsp. **black poppy seed,** ¼ tsp. **sweet paprika,** a sprinkle of **caraway seed.** (4)

BRANDY MACAROON CREAM

Whip ¼ **pint thick cream** till stiff. Add **beaten yolk of 1 fresh egg, 4 tsp. fine sugar, 1 tbs. strong brandy.** Fold in lightly.

Arrange miniature **macaroons** in the bottoms of individual glass bowls. Pour in the brandy cream. Top with a few more macaroons. Chill for ½ hour before serving. (3-4)

Ethics are complete, profound and alive
only when addressed to all living beings.

SCHWEITZER
(Brussels, 1959)

Russia

The mushrooms were of the noblest
quality, pale brown and lightly mottled,
with tapering stalks and conical caps
like those the Tatars wear . . .

Tale of the Three Baba Yagas

MUSHROOM PÂTÉ

The Baba Yaga, that curious old woman of Russian fable who
lived in a house perched on hen's feet, was not remarkable for
her gifts of cookery. In fact, she was more frequently occupied in
thwarting the plans of the virtuous and goodly. Nevertheless,
her knowledge of the forest was uncanny, particularly when it
came to mushrooms, and she was a past master in the preparation of potions and aphrodisiacs. There is something of the
Baba Yaga's witchery in the recipe that follows, so pungently
earthy, so rich and strange does it seem.

Fry **2 tbs. finely-minced sweet onion** in **1 tbs. butter,**
slowly, till the onion turns translucent, together with ¼ **tsp.**
mixed pickling spice (minus the chilli peppers). Then add
¼ **lb. of very finely chopped button mushrooms, a small**
crushed clove of garlic, a scant tsp. of **sea-salt.** Continue
frying gently for a further 5 minutes.

Meanwhile, soak a ½-inch-thick slice of crustless **rye bread** in
cold milk. Squeeze the liquid out of the bread and crumble it
into the pan. Stir through and fry another 2–3 minutes.
Remove pan from heat.

Quickly add ½ **tsp. butter, 1 tsp. cream,** ⅛ **tsp. lemon**
juice, 1 tsp. Instant Soup stock.* Transfer mixture to a
mortar, pound and amalgamate as thoroughly as possible. Pass
the mixture through the mesh of a fine sieve. Discard any
residue which finally remains in the sieve—onion, pickling
spice, etc.

* For "stock" it is advisable to increase the usual amount of Instant Soup
powder (compare p. 15). In this case a solution made up from a scant ½ tsp.
to ¼ cup freshly boiled water is suggested.

Chill the pâté for at least 10 hours before using—it will last 3–4 days if kept cold. Serve spread on extra thin slices of **buttered rye bread.** (Traditionally accompanied by glasses of sweet Champagne.)

MOUZHIK'S CAVIAR

Char a firm, medium size **aubergine (8–10 oz.)** in the flame of a gas cooker, or directly on the electric element—medium hot in either case. Turn from time to time until the entire skin is blackened and flaky—both sides and bottom—and the vegetable is becoming somewhat shrivelled looking. Remove from heat (by holding on to the stalk) and carefully rub off the burnt skin under cold running water. Place on a chopping board, allow to become cool, cut open lengthwise, remove as many seeds as possible, remove stalk.

Add **2 tbs. fried Spanish onion,** a generous sprinkling of **chopped fresh dill (or 1 tsp. crumbled dry), sea-salt, 2 tbs. cider vinegar, 1½ tbs. olive oil, the yolk of a hard-boiled egg, 3 stoned black olives.**

Chop all the ingredients until the mixture achieves the consistency of a very thick purée. Chill before serving on **crackers or canapé biscuits,** and accompany with Katinka cocktails: equal parts of **sweetened fresh orange juice** and **ice-cold vodka,** topped with crushed ice.

YABLONCHIKI POTATOES

Boil firm **potatoes** in their skins till *just* tender—not till they're threatening to come apart. Cool, peel, and chop coarsely.

Have ready some **fresh-grated horseradish**—about 2 tbs. per lb. of potatoes. (Grate the horseradish near an open window—the fumes can be quite powerful.)

Combine the potatoes with the grated horseradish, **sea-salt,** some chopped **fresh dill** (if available), and dress with a thin coating of **sour cream—yoghourt** will do nicely in its stead.

This dish goes extremely well with a salad of thick ripe **tomato slices,** crisp **lettuce hearts** and thin sliced **cucumber,** seasoned with **olive oil, wine vinegar** and **sea-salt.** Serve, too, with a plate of sliced Klops.

KLOPS

A typical Russian-Jewish savoury, often eaten on sabbaths or festive holidays, and easily prepared with a tin of wheat gluten (meatless steaks).

Drain the contents of **1 large tin gluten.** Squeeze each piece very dry in absorbent paper. Mince through the grinder into a bowl—mince fine.

Add **2 beaten eggs, 1–2 large crushed cloves of garlic, 2 tbs. fine matzo meal, 1 tsp. sea-salt, ½ tsp. mixed pickling spice** crushed fine in a mortar.

Soak a **½-inch-thick slice of bread** in water for a few minutes, squeeze out well, crumble into the bowl.

Mix all ingredients very thoroughly and mould into a loaf shape. Place in a very well-oiled loaf tin, sprinkle the top with **paprika,** and bake in a moderate oven (375°—Gas 5) for 30–40 minutes, or until the top is crisp and nicely brown. Remove Klops from tin carefully and let cool on a wire rack. Serve cold, cut in thick slices, with **mustard**—and **Yablon-chiki Potatoes.** (Serves 4)

POTATO AND MUSHROOM ZHARKOYE

Although Russians do not as a rule use soy sauce in their cooking, its use in some Russian dishes does for some inexplicable reason produce an authentic tasting gravy.

Boil **1½ lb. potatoes** in very little water until tender but still firm. Drain and steam in the pan a few moments till really dry, then peel and mash smoothly. Keep very warm.

Heat **1 tbs. peanut** or **sunflower-seed oil** in a heavy frying pan. Add **½ lb. coarsely chopped mushrooms** together with **2 tbs. minced sweet onion** and a crushed clove of **garlic.** Cook gently for about 2 minutes. Increase heat, add **2–3 tbs. soy sauce,** blend everything together well, allow bottom of the pan to become richly brown and tacky. Then add **½ cup cold water,** stir through, cook for 2 minutes longer. Finally, stir in **2 tbs. sour cream** (or yoghourt).

Pour mushrooms and gravy over potatoes, mix lightly, serve. Very nice with a tangy dish of **sauerkraut,** or **Dill-Pickled Cucumbers.** (Serves 4–6)

CAULIFLOWER AND POTATO ZHARKOYE

Boil **1½ lb. potatoes** as above, cool, peel, cut into thick slices.

Chop flowerets of a very small **cauliflower** rather fine and fry in **1½ tbs. vegetable shmaltz** (p. 150) for 5 minutes, together with a crushed clove of **garlic.** Stir from time to time. Add **2–3 tbs. soy sauce,** distribute well throughout the pan, then cover and cook gently for a further 3 minutes. Increase heat, add ½ **cup cold water** and, as a rich frothy gravy forms, the slices of potato. Reduce heat, cover again, simmer 5 minutes longer. (Serves 4–5)

CLEAR MUSHROOM SOUP

The secret of this admirable soup is sheer prodigality. One must think in terms of proverbial Russian hospitality—to do it, to overdo it, what matter, so long as the guests are honoured and happy.

To **2 pints fresh boiling water** add 1½ **tsp. vegetable shmaltz** and simmer for a minute or two. Then one chopped **spring onion** and **1 lb. mushrooms,** cleaned and sliced fine. Simmer for 5 minutes, then add **sea-salt** and fresh ground **black pepper.** Put cover half on, cook slowly for a further 25 minutes. (Serves 5–6)

POTATO AND SPRING ONION SOUP

After the guests have left, and with them most of the choicer things in the larder, there is still opportunity for ingenuity . . .

To **2 pints water** add **1 tsp. vegetable shmaltz** and **6 chopped spring onions.** Bring to the boil and add **3 large peeled potatoes** cut into small cubes. Simmer until potatoes are very tender and can be broken easily with a fork. Season with **salt** and freshly ground **black pepper** and more shmaltz if desired. Serve with thick slices of **black bread and butter.** (4)

SMETANA SALAD

A refreshingly different summer luncheon plate—substantial in itself—particularly welcome when the day is hot and the thought of cooking is oppressive.

Into a large salad bowl tear **2 well-washed lettuces.** Add slices of **radish, cucumber, sweet green pepper, tomato, spring onions, raw button mushrooms,** plus a handful of **chopped fresh dill** and a sprinkling of **crushed walnuts.** Swirl through generously with **sour cream** or **smetana** (a thinned down version of sour cream) and season with **sea-salt.** Accompany with thick slices of **rye bread and butter.** (4–6)

HALUSHKI

In districts round Poltava, and elsewhere, perhaps, men and boys used to make themselves sick at *halushki*-eating contests.

Boil ¾ **lb. potatoes** till soft. Cool, peel and mash thoroughly.

Add: **1 egg, 1 tsp. sea-salt, 6 tbs. flour.** Mix together to a smooth pliable dough. Place on a well-floured board, place a small sheet of polythene on top, roll out to $\frac{1}{4}$ inch thickness. Cut into small rounds, about $1\frac{1}{2}$ inch diameter, drop carefully into a large saucepan with plenty of boiling salted water. Cook about 5–7 minutes, skim out, drain. Toss with **butter,** and, when it melts, with **sour cream** and a little **chopped parsley.** Serve hot. (2–3)

DILL-PICKLED CUCUMBERS

For this recipe you will need the firm **"ridge" cucumbers** which are generally available during August and September. You will also need a rather large amount of **fresh dill** (see note at end of recipe), which is obtainable during the same period. This is the time when dill reaches its full maturity, and yellow flowers appear on the stalks.

First sterilize your preserving jars and have them ready ($1\frac{1}{2}$ pint jars).

Wash and lightly scrub cucumbers thoroughly, removing any sand or grit. Put aside for fresh eating any which are not perfectly sound or hard. Fill the jars with as many cucumbers as possible, standing them on end, and fitting them in snugly together.

Into each jar drop **1–2 halved cloves of garlic, 2 slices carrot** cut lengthwise, and **half a celery stalk,** plus $1\frac{1}{2}$ **tsp. mixed pickling spice.**

Stuff the mouth of each jar with a good-sized bunch of dill which has been well washed first.

Now make up your pickling solution: for each cup of cold water use **1 tbs. sea-salt.** Prepare a large pitcher of this solution and stir well till the salt is completely dissolved.

Fill the jars with the brine till they are overflowing slightly, cap down immediately and close very tight.

If you want the pickling process to be speedy, leave in a warm exposed position—they will be ready to sample in about 7–10 days. Otherwise, store in a cool dry larder for extended keeping—they will last throughout the winter if kept this way.

Some dilled cucumber experts claim that it is preferable to turn the jars upside down during the initial pickling process, that is, for the first 5 days or so, thereafter to turn them right side up for the remaining time until they are opened.

In either case, there will be a slight leakage from the jars after the first 2–3 days. This is quite normal as fermentation begins to set in, but it soon leaves off.

Note: If fresh dill is unobtainable, proceed in exactly the same way without the dill. The cucumbers will still be delightful.

KASHA

Kasha, or **buckwheat groats,** is a wonderfully versatile grain, much used in central Russia and the Ukraine. It is usually prepared in the same way as rice. A few tablespoons of cooked Kasha added to clear soup give depth and a characteristic extra flavour. It is delicious combined with cooked pastas, particularly the bowknot kind (see p. 161). It also makes an excellent supper on its own mixed with fried onion and fresh cottage cheese.

To make plain Kasha: wash a cup of the grain and put to boil in **1¾ cups cold water** and **½ tsp. sea-salt.** Reduce heat and simmer, covered, until all the water is absorbed and the grains are tender without being mushy. Stir occasionally. (As with rice, you will have to gauge the temperament of your Kasha—usually 1¾ cups of water are ample, but you may need a tiny bit more.) Steam on the side of the cooker for 5–10 minutes longer. To serve, simply add butter and a little more sea-salt.

For roasted Kasha: put a cup of Kasha, unwashed, into a hot, unoiled frying pan. Shake the pan frequently and dry-fry over a medium heat for about 5–7 minutes. Now add **2½–3 cups cold water,** let it froth to a light boil, then reduce heat to a simmer and cook as above for plain Kasha. When done, add **1 tbs. vegetable shmaltz** plus a sprinkling of **sea-salt** and **pepper.**

KASHA AND RED CABBAGE

Simmer **1 cup Kasha** in **1¾ cups Instant Soup solution,** until each grain is tender. Leave on a warm part of the cooker to continue steaming.

Heat **1 tbs. peanut oil** in a large pan, add in **1½ cups fine shredded red cabbage** and cook gently for 3 minutes, stirring from time to time. Now add **1½–2 tbs. soy sauce, a small crushed clove of garlic,** a light sprinkling of **sea-salt.** Continue cooking another 4 minutes, stirring as before. Increase heat, add **¼ cup cold water** and **2 tbs. vodka** (optional) and cook vigorously for 2 minutes longer. Remove from heat.

The cabbage, when done, should still have most of the crisp juicy texture of the raw vegetable.

Combine cabbage and Kasha thoroughly and serve topped with generous dollops of **sour cream**. (4–6)

KASHA AND BABY MARROWS (COURGETTES)

Heat a very small amount of **peanut oil** in a heavy frying pan. When smoking hot, add in **3 chopped spring onions** and a large crushed clove of **garlic**. Within 30 seconds remove onion and garlic from pan and set aside.

Have a **thin batter mixture** ready (see Mixed Fritters p. 24).

Slice **5 baby marrows (8–10 oz.)** each into 4 slices lengthwise. Reheat pan with **2 tbs. peanut oil.** Coat each marrow slice in batter and fry till both sides are crisp and brown. Drain on absorbent paper, **salt** lightly, sprinkle over with the spring onion/garlic mixture. Keep hot.

Add a little more oil to the pan, pour in **1¾ cups cold water** plus **1 tbs. soy sauce.** Bring to the boil. Decrease heat and stir in **2 tbs. gooseberry jam** (or **red-currant**), and a cup of washed **Kasha.** Cover and cook gently as for plain Kasha.

Serve Kasha on a large heated platter, surrounded by the fried marrows, and with a topping over all of a generous sprinkling of **toasted, slivered almonds.** (4–6)

FLAVOURY RADISHES

Peel and slice **a large black radish** (see p. 96) into very thin rounds. If you can't get black radish, large firm red ones will do. Sprinkle well with **sea-salt** and coat with a small amount of **vegetable shmaltz.** Excellent as an instant relish.

SWEET AND SOUR POTATOES

Cook **1½ lb. potatoes** till *just* tender. Cool, peel and cut into small chunks.

Heat **1½ tbs. vegetable shmaltz** in a heavy pan. Add **1 medium size chopped onion,** fry till light golden. Reduce heat. Add **1 tbs. soy sauce** and fry a minute longer, then **2 tbs. cold water.** Now **5 skinned, cored and chopped tomatoes** (10 oz.) plus a large crushed clove of **garlic** and **1½ tsp. sea-salt.** Stir and simmer gently 10 minutes. Finally, add the juice of a large **lemon** and **2½-3 tbs. demerara sugar.** Stir again, simmer 5-7 minutes longer.

Now put in the potatoes, mix through, and cook a little more, till potatoes are completely tender and have absorbed a certain amount of the juices. (Serves 4-5)

SAUERKRAUT

Sauerkraut is not only an extremely tasty side-dish but a very digestible and healthful food as well. There are literally dozens of different ways of presenting it, each with a subtly different flavour from before. Sauerkraut can be bought loose in many continental food shops, most of the year round. The tinned variety is never as good. Combinations that follow are for **1 lb. sauerkraut.**

Sauerkraut and swelled raisins

Plump **2 tbs. seedless raisins** in freshly boiled water for 10-12 minutes or till well expanded. Drain and add to plain **sauerkraut** together with **olive oil, wine vinegar** and a light sprinkling of **sea-salt.** Mix well through and chill before serving.

Apple Sauerkraut

Grate a **sweet crisp apple** into the sauerkraut, add **2 tsp. lemon juice, 1 tbs. olive oil** and a light dusting of **sugar.** Blend well and chill.

Green Sauerkraut

Add **1 tbs. minced sweet onion, 1 tbs. chopped fresh herb (basil, dill, parsley or borage), 1 tbs. olive oil,** a sprinkling of **sea-salt.**

Cranberry Sauerkraut

Bruise **6-8 fresh cranberries** and add to the sauerkraut, together with ½ **tsp. fine sugar** and **1 tbs. olive oil.** Leave covered in refrigerator for 24 hours.

Caraway Sauerkraut

Mix sauerkraut with ½ **tsp. caraway seed,** ¼ **cup finely shredded carrot** and **1 tbs. olive oil.**

Yoghourt Sauerkraut

Add **6 tbs. yoghourt** to sauerkraut, mix well and chill.

Sauerkraut and wine

Add ½ **cup good, medium dry, red wine.** Mix well and chill.

The above are only a few of the varied ways in which sauerkraut can be treated. You can try other ingredients with it: **shelled young peas, grated raw beetroot, thin sliced raw button mushrooms, sweet green pepper, spring onions,** etc.

HERMIT'S BREAD

Take a wide slab of **rye bread.** Dip a juicy clove of **garlic** repeatedly in **sea-salt** as you rub it briskly into and around the crust. Butter thickly, cover with slices of **cucumber** and **fresh-cut dill,** sprinkle with more sea-salt.

CHERRY DUMPLINGS

Wash and stone **1 lb. medium sweet cherries.** Add to a saucepan together with **3 oz. demerara sugar** and ½ **cup cold water.** Bring to a light boil and simmer gently 12–15 minutes. Skim surface.

Make up a fairly thick dumpling batter: **4 oz. plain flour** sifted with ½ **tsp. baking powder** and ¼ **tsp. sea-salt,** then mixed lightly together with ½ **cup milk.**

Drop batter by spoonfuls into the simmering cherries and syrup. After it is all in, shake the pan and continue simmering, with the cover half on, for about 10 minutes. Now turn all the dumplings carefully over, put the cover full on, and continue simmering for 20 minutes more. Shake the pan from time to time. Serve hot or cold with **sour cream, sweet cream** or **plain yoghourt.** (Enough for 4)

> Love the animals, love the plants, love everything.
>
> DOSTOIEVSKY
> (*The Brothers Karamazov*)

Scandinavia

The Earl of Sandwich is said to have invented the sandwich. Without wishing to quibble over this well-known fact, it would have been simpler all round had it been labelled the *closed* or *portable* sandwich. Because certain Danes, in the folk-lore line, laugh this off with other nations' "so-called firsts". Their claim is that the smörgåsbrod or *open* sandwiches of Scandinavia are part of a tradition lost in the mists of time. Were they due, one wonders, to the ingenuity of neat-minded Viking ladies, appalled at the mess their husbands made getting up suddenly from over-laden tables? As we know, Vikings were always moving off at short notice. We learn nothing of this, nor anything about the portable sandwich either, which, in any case, would have been a hindrance in time of battle. To have any kind of sandwich in one hand and a flailing broadsword in the other would inevitably have affected discipline. War, after all, is a pretty poor dish for all men. The original smörgåsbrod, we may suspect, were laid out on slabs of coarse barley bread. The contemporary ones are all that refinement and good taste could require.

Smörgåsbrod (Sweden) or Smørbrød (Norway) or Smørrebrød (Denmark) are attractively prepared open face sandwiches on a bed of rye bread, buttered, and topped over with layers of tasty ingredients. Two or three of them with a glass of cold Lager are an ample luncheon or dinner, and a delight to any Viking or non-Viking eye.

To prepare Smörgåsbrod: butter thin slices of **rye or pumpernickel bread** (the latter available in most delicatessen shops); have ready a large bowl of washed, drained and chilled **lettuce leaves;** after you have made up a selection of toppings and garnishes from the 40-odd that follow, apply a bed of lettuce leaves to the bread and carry on:

(1) Mash a ripe or overripe **avocado** to purée. Flavour with a little **mayonnaise, chilli powder, sea-salt, lemon juice.** Spread over the lettuce. Top with **ripe tomato quarters,** a few **black olive halves,** a sprig of **fresh dill.**

(2) Add a little **cream or top milk** to **cottage cheese** and mash smooth. Blend with a little **paprika** to produce a light pinky colour, then fold in some **chopped chives** and **minced dill-pickled cucumber.** Spread over the lettuce, decorate with thin circlets of **red radish** and a few **pickled baby beets.**

(3) **Hard-boiled eggs** mashed smooth and mixed with **vegetable shmaltz, sea-salt, fresh ground pepper, lemon juice, minced sweet onion.** Then spread over the lettuce and decorated with **sweet red pepper rings.**

(4) **A small tin of beans in tomato sauce,** drained, then dressed in **yoghourt** with an admixture of a little **salt, chopped spring onion, chopped and seeded green chilli pepper.** Cover with slices of **tinned celery hearts** and a sprinkling of **lemon juice.**

(5) Core a firm **cucumber** and discard seedy centre. Stuff with a mixture of **cream cheese** and **chopped sweet pimento,** moistened with **sherry.** Chill for a few hours beforehand. Then cut into thick slices and arrange over the lettuce. Finish with coarsely crushed **toasted almonds** and **radish roses.**

(6) **Cooked or tinned chick peas** mashed to a purée, flavoured with **olive oil, lemon juice, garlic salt.** Spread over the lettuce. Cover with **thick tomato slices** previously marinated in **wine vinegar** for a few minutes. Decorate with a **sprig of parsley.**

(7) A thick layer of **"Taramasalata"** (p. 132), and on top of it **whole capers** and **coarsely chopped green olives,** and on top of that **a large slice of tomato** decked out with **dry crumbled basil.** Serve with **lemon wedges.**

(8) A thick layer of **peanut butter** over the lettuce, followed by a layer of **sweet onion rings.** Then **cucumber rounds** and **green olive halves.** A topping of **chopped fresh coriander leaves.**

(9) Four or five slices of **Cold Breaded Gluten** (p. 87) arranged over the lettuce with small **cherry tomato halves,** and flanked by **wedges of lemon** and **pickled pearl onions.**

(10) Coarsely chopped, skinned ripe **tomatoes,** flavoured with **olive oil** and **garlic salt** and arranged over the lettuce. Over it, horse-shoe slices of ripe **avocado,** and in their semi-circles **large black olives.** Squeeze over with **lemon juice.**

(11) Mix a small amount of **fresh grated horseradish** with **cream cheese.** Season with a little **lemon juice.** Spread.

Cover with **strips of length-cut cucumber, sweet pimento strips,** a sprinkling of **dry dill or basil.** Drizzle lightly with **olive oil.**

(12) **Sliced hard-boiled egg** as a first layer. Slices of **pickled mushroom** as a second. **Chopped parsley** and **tiny red radishes** on top.

(13) Cover the lettuce with a layer of **cottage cheese.** Make a well in the centre. Fill well and mound up with finely grated raw vegetables like: **cauliflower, carrot, celery, beetroot**—already dressed with **mayonnaise** and **lemon juice.** Decorate with **watercress.**

(14) A layer of **"Chopped Herring without Herring"** (p. 114). Then slices of length-cut **dill-pickled cucumber, pickled onion rings** and a few **pecan halves** on top.

(15) **A thick slice of cheese;** on top of it a small mound of **sauerkraut** mellowed in **olive oil** and seasoned with **sea-salt.** Frame with **tomato quarters** on each of the sides, **black olives** in the corners.

(16) **Cottage cheese** mixed in with lots of **brown-fried onion** and flavoured with **coriander powder** and **sea-salt.** On top of it, alternate strips of **celery heart** and **sweet red peppers,** ½ inch apart.

(17) A layer of **Pickled Carrots** (p. 151) over the lettuce, followed by a layer of **sliced hard-boiled egg.** On top, halves of bland **black olives.**

(18) Slices of **green tomato** fried in a little **vegetable shmaltz** together with some lightly crushed **coriander seed** and **sea-salt.** Cooled, then put in a single layer over the lettuce. Top with cubes of **cheese** dotted over with **cayenne pepper.** Serve with an accompaniment of **olives.**

(19) Dice **cold boiled potatoes** and mix with **chopped spring onion.** Toss in **mayonnaise** sharpened with **wine vinegar.** Pile generously over the lettuce. Decorate with **sliced pickled gherkins** and thin slices of **pickled beetroot.**

(20) Cut tops off firm smallish **tomatoes** and scoop out the centres. Chop centres together with a little **sweet green pepper, salt** and a few **walnuts.** Fill tomatoes with this mixture, decorate with **almond-stuffed green olives.** Allow 2–3 tomatoes per sandwich.

(21) Whip **cream cheese** through with a little **top milk** and flavour with **caraway seed.** Form into small balls and arrange, 4–5 per sandwich, over the lettuce. In between the

cheese place chunks or cubes of **tinned pineapple.** Decorate with a few fresh **mint leaves.**

(22) A row of sliced **Pickled Mushrooms** (p. 133) down the centre of the lettuce. The top halves of **tinned green asparagus** arranged on either side of it. Strips of **red pimento** between the stalks of asparagus. Drizzle over with **lemon juice** and **olive oil.**

(23) Make up very small **Burgers** (p. 116), allow about 4 to a sandwich. Top with **pickled onion rings,** and in their centres a slice of **pickled red or green chilli pepper.**

(24) Chop **hard-boiled eggs** together with a few tender **watercress leaves.** Add a dressing of **olive oil, lemon juice, salt** and prepared **mustard.** Spread over the lettuce. Top with strips of **pimento** and some **green olive halves.**

(25) A layer of **thick tomato slices** over the lettuce and a grating of **Geska cheese** on top. Then wedges of ripe **avocado** with a light dusting of **sea-salt** and a squeeze of **lemon juice.** Finally, a swirl of **Green Aioli** (p. 57) running down the centre.

(26) Cut medium size **sweet red peppers** into halves lengthwise. Remove pith and seeds. Fill cavities with **cottage cheese** blended through with **chopped fresh dill, diced black olives, diced cucumber, salt,** and a binding of **sour cream.** Allow half a stuffed pepper per sandwich. Decorate with **pimento-stuffed green olives** and **watercress.**

(27) Slice **cheese** into matchstick slivers. Blend with a little **salad cream** and flavour with **paprika** and **chopped capers.** Strew over lettuce. Top with slices of **pickled beetroot** and **onion.** Decorate with wispy **fennel leaves.**

(28) The top halves of **tinned asparagus** and **tinned sweet-corn kernels** sautéed in **olive oil** for a few minutes, together with a bruised **garlic clove.** Then garlic removed and mixture cooled and spread over the lettuce, flavoured with a squeeze of **lemon juice** and a sprinkling of **black pepper.** Garnish with fine strips of **sweet red pepper.**

(29) A layer of **Mushroom Pâté** (p. 61) over the lettuce, decorated with **blanched fried almond halves** and a few **green olives.**

(30) Razor-thin slices of **black radish,** mellowed in **salt** and **vegetable shmaltz,** then arranged over the lettuce. Cover with **quarters of hard-boiled egg** sprinkled over with **paprika.** A few slivers of length-cut **spring onion** on top.

(31) A mélange of **sliced tomato, cucumber, radish** and

celery tossed in **olive oil, wine vinegar, salt** and a liberal grating of **Geska cheese,** then arranged over the lettuce.

(32) Add a little **sour cream** or **yoghourt** to **bryndza cheese.** Beat till light and creamy, pile on the lettuce. Top with **dill-pickled cucumber rounds** (p. 65) and slices of **pickled pepper** (p. 79).

(33) Thin slices of **sweet Spanish onion,** mellowed in **olive oil** and **sea-salt** for 15 minutes, then mixed with **yoghourt** and **paprika** and spread over the lettuce. Top with lots of **chopped parsley,** and over that slices of **large black olives.**

(34) Mix chunks of **cold boiled potato** with **Skordalia** (p. 135) and spread over the lettuce. Top with **grated raw beetroot** dressed with **olive oil, wine vinegar** and **sea-salt.** Sprinkle over lightly-toasted **sunflower seeds.**

(35) The inner stalks from a head of crisp **celery,** washed, their hollows filled with a combination of **bryndza cheese** (softened if necessary with some **cream or yoghourt**), **chopped pickled beetroot** and **pecans.** Cut into halves and put 2 or 3 on each sandwich. Fill in between with **pickled capers,** decorate with **mustard and cress.**

(36) **Thick slices of tomato** dressed with **olive oil, sea-salt** and **chopped fresh basil.** Cover with tiny boiled **new potatoes** tossed in **melted butter** and **chopped fresh dill.** Decorate with coarsely minced **green olives.**

(37) **Tinned or fresh-cooked artichoke hearts,** sliced thick and dressed with **Green Aioli** (p. 57). Top with **tomato rounds,** decorate with **chopped fresh tarragon, radish roses.**

(38) A thick layer of **Goldy Green Spread** (p. 115) over the lettuce. Decorate with slices of **celery stalk, chopped toasted almonds, fresh "ridge" cucumber rounds** and a sprig of **fresh dill.**

(39) Fry all together, with a flavouring of **sea-salt,** some **chopped skinned tomatoes, diced sweet green pepper, chopped sweet onion,** till onion is slightly softened. Cool and spread over the lettuce. Top with **large black olive halves** and a few **mint leaves.**

(40) Beat a ripe or overripe **avocado** to a creamy mass, blend with a sieved **hard-boiled egg.** Add a little **lemon juice, salt, dry mustard** and **olive oil.** Pile in a mound in the centre of the lettuce. Surround with a rim of **cottage cheese** combined with a few **cummin seeds** and **toasted crushed almonds.** Decorate with leaves of **watercress.**

Central Europe

> ... there is no virtue, no instinct in the
> human heart which does not find analogy
> in the world of animals.
>
> HERDER

GULYAS FALUDI

A full-throated dish, worthy of a flourish of violins (preferably Gypsy), soft candlelight and a good rich wine.

peel **7 shallots** but leave whole
cut **1 lb. peeled potatoes** into medium size chunks
slice **4 oz. young carrots** into rounds
seed **1 red or green sweet pepper,** medium size (4 oz.), and cut into large pieces
blanch **4 medium size tomatoes** in very hot water, then skin, core, discard seeds, sprinkle over with ½ **tsp. demerara sugar**
slice **4 oz. tart cooking apple**
chop **1½ oz. Spanish onion**
have ready **4 good sized cloves of garlic,** ½ **tsp. mixed pickling spice,** a crumbled **bay-leaf**

In an earthenware casserole, **in 2 tbs. vegetable shmaltz** (see p. 150), fry the shallots and chopped onion, together with the pickling spice and bay-leaf. Turn the shallots frequently till they become somewhat glazed and light golden. Add the garlic, crushed, and the green or red pepper. Stir and fry a further 5 minutes on a medium heat. Now add the potatoes, carrots, tomatoes and apple, plus **2 tsp. sea-salt, 1½ tsp. paprika,** ½ **tsp. demerara sugar** and ½ **cup Instant Soup solution.**

Mix vegetables thoroughly, cover, transfer casserole to oven, bake at medium heat (325°—Gas 3) for about 2 hours.

Serve with plenty of cold **sour cream** or **plain yoghourt** for swirling through the cooking juices. (Serves 4)

Finish with lemon tea and Quick Deep Strudel.

QUICK DEEP STRUDEL

Combine **3 oz. matzo meal** with **2 oz. butter.** Blend the butter through the meal with the fingers till the whole is a fine crumble. Then add **2 oz. soft light-brown sugar** and ⅛ **tsp. cinnamon.** Mix well.

In a fairly deep, medium size glass casserole, tamp a thin layer of the crumble mixture over the bottom. Tamp firmly. Do likewise round the sides, until about three-quarters the way up. Fill in with: **12 oz. finely sliced tart apple,** blended with ½ **oz. almonds** and ½ **oz. walnuts** (both crushed fine), ½ **tsp. grated lemon rind,** ¼ **tsp. cinnamon,** 2–3 **tbs. soft light-brown sugar.**

Sprinkle over with the remaining crumble mixture. Bake in a moderate oven (350°—Gas 4) for about 45 minutes, or till the top turns nicely brown. Serve hot with lashings of cold **sour cream.** (4)

BABUSHKA'S CELEBRATION SOUP

Customs Officer, to aged peasant woman (in the days when the boundary between Poland and Russia was frequently in dispute):

"Well, Granny, they've redrawn the border again, so now your little house is back in Poland."

Aged peasant woman: "Ah, thank the Lord, my dear, I couldn't have borne another of those freezing Russian winters."

Saying which, she went humming into her garden and picked

1 medium size leek
some **celeriac (3 oz.)**
1 jerusalem artichoke (2 oz.)
1 young parsnip (2 oz.)
1 medium size carrot
1 medium size potato

She put them in her apron, went inside, laid them out on the table and added a slice of **white cabbage (2 oz.).** Everything was then washed to get rid of earth or sand, and, except for the leek and cabbage, everything was peeled.

Babushka chopped all the vegetables very fine. This done, **2 tsp. olive oil** and **1 tsp. butter** were heated in a heavy saucepan. The vegetables were then added and allowed to "sweat" over a low heat for 5 minutes. Then a **crushed clove of garlic** went in along with 2¼ **tsp. sea-salt.** Everything was stirred and cooked another 2 minutes, before **2 pints hot water** were poured in slowly. The heat was turned well up until the soup came to the boil, then down again for a half-hour of slow simmering, with the cover half-on, half-off. After which Babushka tasted it to check the seasoning, and put the soup through a fine sieve. It was then returned to the saucepan, rewarmed a bit, and served up in big bowls with a platter of **spring onions** and plenty of **rye bread and butter.**

Of course, Babushka invited the Customs Officer—and two of his friends—to join her.

GREEN TOMATO OMELETTE

The custom of pickling green tomatoes is as old as that of cucumbers. The reason is obvious: until they're ripe or pickled they are quite inedible. But here is a method of enjoying their delightful "greeny" flavour in a thoroughly digestible way.

For 4 portions, buy **1 lb. small, completely green tomatoes.** They are frequently available if you ask for them. Cut each into quarters. Chop **4 shallots** coarsely. In a frying pan heat **2–3 tbs. vegetable shmaltz,** add the shallots, fry till pale golden. Add the tomatoes, along with **1 tsp. crushed coriander seed** and a sprinkling of **sea-salt,** cook on a low heat 10 minutes, stirring occasionally. Remove onions and tomatoes to a bowl and keep warm.

Now make your omelettes—**2 eggs per person.** When done, slide out on to hot plates, distribute the green tomato/onion mixture generously over them, fold over. Serve immediately.

STUFFED POTATO BAKE

Heat **2 tbs. olive oil** in a small pan, fry **1 tbs. chopped onion** in it till golden. Then add: **1 medium carrot,** grated fine, **2 oz. pulverized almonds** (through the electric grinder), **2 crushed garlic cloves,** ¼ tsp. **chopped parsley, 1 tsp. sea-salt.** Fry gently, stirring often, for 5–7 minutes. Set aside.

Put **1 tbs. olive oil** in a deep casserole. Line the bottom with **2 oz. sweet onion rings.** Add a few thin **carrot slices,** ¼ tsp. **coriander seed,** a **crushed clove of garlic.** Simmer gently on top of the cooker for about 7 minutes.

Meanwhile, peel **1½ lb. medium size potatoes,** and hollow out the centres, generously, all the way through. Discard the cores or use for Babushka's Celebration Soup. Fill the potatoes with the carrot/almond mixture, leaving about ¼ inch unfilled at either end. Arrange in the casserole, dust well with sea-salt and a little fresh ground **black pepper.** If there is any stuffing left over, strew it on the potatoes.

Cut **2 medium size tomatoes** into quarters, sprinkle with **sugar,** place in the casserole around the potatoes.

Mix **1 tsp. paprika** with **8 tbs. plain yoghourt.** Pour the mixture over everything, cover the casserole. Bake at 350–375° (Gas 4–5) for 1½ hours. About 15 minutes before the end, uncover and continue baking till potatoes are golden and tender. (Serves 3–4)

MUSLEENA BUTTER

Put **2 oz. (after stoning) bland, ripe black olives** through a fine mincer. Add to them:

½ **tsp. spring onion**—minced very fine (green stems only)
½ **tsp. celery**—minced
⅛ **tsp. paprika**
scant ⅛ **tsp. caraway powder** (ground caraway seed)
1 tsp. dry red wine (or **sherry**)
1 tsp. sea-salt
a crushed sliver of **garlic**

Mix all the ingredients together very well, then add **2 tbs. softened butter.** Blend as thoroughly as possible and chill in the refrigerator. Serve thinly spread over **thin buttered toast or melba toast.** Sprinkle with **lemon juice** or accompany with **lemon wedges.** Use up the same day.

POLISH LUNCHEON PLATTER

Polanders are passionately fond of dill-pickled cucumbers. They chop them into soups, eat them with plain rye bread and butter or with bryndza cheese, or just nibble them while drinking lemon tea. Here is what Romain Gary, who spent most of his childhood and part of his youth in Poland, has to say of pickled cucumbers:

"I often buy a pound at a time, then settle down somewhere in the sun, preferably on the ocean shore, or on the pavement, no matter where, and munch my cucumbers. These are my only moments of bliss . . . If the landscape is beautiful, so much the better; while I look at it, eating my pickled cucumbers, I feel that I am eating it too. It is a good way of taking possession of the world. Give me a pound of [them] and I know that life is worth living, that happiness *is* attainable."*

And after that, it's almost inelegant to add:

Hard-boil **6 eggs,** cool and shell. Cut each into half lengthwise and remove yolks to a bowl. Mash. Add ½ **small dill-pickled cucumber,** fine chopped, enough good **salad cream** to bind, ¼ **tsp. paprika, sea-salt** and **pepper** to taste. Mix well and pile back into the egg whites. Set them in the middle of a large platter and surround with: a thick bed of **shredded lettuce** leaves dotted over with **fresh chopped dill,** and, on top, more dilled cucumber, divided into quarters; lots of boiled **new potatoes** sprinkled over with **lemon juice** and **paprika** and fresh chopped dill; thick slices of **ripe tomato;** young **spring onions;** whole young **radishes;** raw young **green beans** sliced diagonally and thin.

Let everyone help themselves from the central platter to their own plates. Provide cruets of **olive oil** and **wine vinegar,** a generous pot of **sour cream,** a stack of **bread and butter.** Serve with glasses of cold lager. (4–6)

PAULA'S PICKLED PEPPERS

When, during August and September, sweet green and red peppers are more plentiful and cheap, it is time to make up this superb appetizer:

Wash **1–2 lb. sweet peppers,** dry them, put them directly on the elements of your electric cooker on a medium heat, or over medium gas flames. Turn frequently, until the skins are completely charred—all around, and top and bottom. (An aroma like that of pleasant burning leaves will fill your kitchen with its autumnal fragrance.) Remove peppers from heat, by the stalks, slit each open and allow to cool. Rub off the flaky blackened skins under cold running water. Remove stalks and cores, seeds and pith.

Cut peppers into halves, or quarters, place in a deep earthenware crock. Pour over this marinade:

For every cup of water—2½ **tbs. acetic acid, 2 tsp. sea-salt, 2 tbs. demerara sugar.** Stir well till dissolved. Immerse the peppers completely, keep in a cool place, serve after 6–8 hours—with **bread and butter,** or **Polish Luncheon Platter, Stuffed Potato Bake,** or **Fried Gluten and Eggs.**

* From *Promise at Dawn*—Michael Joseph, 1962.

FRIED GLUTEN AND EGGS

Rinse the contents of a **small tin of gluten** (meatless steaks), squeeze out fairly dry. Cut into ¼-inch-thick rounds.

Beat **4 eggs** in a bowl. Pour a little of the beaten egg off into a saucer, and add to it: ½ **tsp. pulverized mixed pickling spice,** ½ **tsp. sea-salt, a small clove of garlic** (crushed). Blend well.

Dip the gluten slices first into the spice/egg mixture, then lightly into **matzo meal.** But do this just before placing them in the pan.

Fry **2 oz. sliced sweet onion** in 2½ **tbs. vegetable shmaltz** (or **olive oil**). When onion begins to colour add the dipped gluten slices, and fry on a medium heat till both sides are crisped and egg-golden.

To the unseasoned beaten eggs add: **1 tbs. matzo meal,** ¾ **tsp. sea-salt.** Stir well, pour over the gluten. Fry till underside of egg is lightly brown in patches, turn, not necessarily in one piece, fry a minute longer. Serve immediately on hot platters with **dill-pickled cucumbers** or **Paula's Pickled Peppers** and **rye bread and butter.** (Serves 2–3) Finish with dried prunes, apricots and almonds, and lemon tea.

CORIANDER CHEESE DIP

To ¾ **lb. cottage or curd cheese** add: ¼ **tsp. paprika, 1 tsp. chopped capers, 2 tbs. cream** or **yoghourt** (more, if the cheese is particularly dry), a sprinkling of **sea-salt, 2–3 tbs. chopped fresh coriander leaves.** Beat well together and pile into a bowl. Serve with thick chunks of **toasted bread.**

> Ich bin ein Sächsischer Bauer,
> Mein Leben wird mir sauer.

Which goes into English roughly as . . . I am a Saxon peasant, my life is most unpleasant. And when we learn that it comes from the period of the Thirty Years' War, we can understand the plaint only too well. Yet, war or no war, life of a kind went on. People even danced and sang occasionally, especially when festive days came round. The festivals were gargantuan affairs— cauldrons of potatoes, cabbage, onions and anything else on hand were baked overnight in the local village oven, and distributed the next day. No doubt, it was at times like these that our Bauer forgot his troubles and ate his fill. Here is an up-to-date version of this more than man-sized supper, especially satisfying on a blustery March evening . . .

BAUERNSPEISE

Prepare

4 oz. sweet carrot—scraped and cut into small chunks
1 lb. peeled potatoes—cut into large dice
2 oz. fresh broad beans—without pods
1 small peeled onion with **4 whole cloves** stuck in it
10 oz. sauerkraut—rinsed well in cold water, then squeezed quite dry

Heat **2 tbs. vegetable shmaltz** in a heavy earthenware casserole. Add the sauerkraut and fork through to separate the strands. Continue frying, and stirring, for about 10 minutes, until sauerkraut is slightly golden. Then add the rest of the vegetables and this seasoning; **1 bay-leaf,** broken in two, **1 large garlic clove,** minced, **⅛ tsp. caraway seed, 1 tsp. demerara sugar,** about **1½ tsp. sea-salt** (or as desired). Mix everything thoroughly, then pour in **¾ cup dry cider** and **¼ cup water.** Keep the carrots submerged if possible. Now sprinkle over with **¼ tsp. paprika** and bake, covered, in a moderate oven (300–325°—Gas 2–3) for 2 hours. If you wish to brown the top, leave cover off for the last 15 minutes. (Serves 4)

And if after you eat it the "peasant" in you is still unsatisfied, go on to this:

PLAIN COUNTRY FRUIT BAKE

Soak **4 oz. dried prunes** and **4 oz. dried apricots**—separately—in freshly boiled water. Soak for ¾ hour. Drain.

Butter a shallow ovenproof dish, cut a **banana** into inch-long sections and arrange over the bottom. Put the soaked fruit in with the banana. Pour over **½ cup sweet cider** in which **2½–3 tbs. mild honey** has been dissolved. Sprinkle in a generous snowfall of **fine grated citrus fruit rind** (lemon, grapefruit, orange or lime). Dot well with butter and bake, uncovered, in a slow oven (300°—Gas 2) for 1½–2 hours, or till the fruit is glazed and tender. Serve with plenty of cold **sour cream, yoghourt** or **sweet cream.**

The forests of central Europe abound in blueberries. A Carpathian tale tells how a youth was ordered to the woods one day to collect a capful of them. But wherever he went, all he could see were red berries or black ones, strawberries or raspberries. And none of those with whom he spoke had heard of the name "blueberries". In desperation he called upon the spirits of the wood to help and one came, in the form of a blue light or luminescence. And wherever the blue light led, the youth followed and found clumps of blueberries. The light led him across Carpathia, Poland, even to the wide lands of Russia, and the youth went on, filling his cap, eating from it greedily, being intoxicated with the flavour. And though the youth never returned to his home, the blueberries flourished. And where the blue light shines sometimes, there they flourish best . . .

GOLDEN BERRY CUSTARD

Wash ½ **lb. blueberries** thoroughly. Put in a 1½–2 pint glass casserole, **sugar** liberally, sprinkle over with **1 tbs. Kirsch.** Blend well.

Make up a custard batter. Put **2 oz. plain flour** into a bowl, add to it **2 eggs** beaten together with **3 tbs. powdered sugar.** Work in well. Then **1 cup milk,** poured in slowly, stirring and beating all the while. Pour over the berries. Bake, uncovered, for 1–1¼ hours (400°—Gas 6) or till custard has set and coloured golden and brown.

Serve chilled, in thick slices.

CHEW-STREW

It used to be commonplace, or so we're told, in many of the city streets of central Europe, to see the remains of melon seed shells scattered about. Of course, this was during the more easy going days before the last war, when such things as public discussion on the pavements and eating melon seeds were carried on—usually simultaneously. The latter habit anyway is a tranquillizing one, but insidious to contract, since once you start nibbling these tasty salty tidbits you seldom leave off— till the last one has gone.

Almost any kind of marrow or melon seed will do—pumpkin (best), squash, vegetable marrow, watermelon. Sunflower too.

Wash seeds well, getting rid of any pith or adhering vegetable matter. Bring well-salted water to the boil, toss the seeds in. Simmer 30–40 minutes. Drain and let dry.

Arrange seeds in a single layer on baking sheets and bake in a very slow oven, turning frequently. They should turn crisp but never brown—a faint beige (pumpkin and marrow) is the optimum colour. Cool, then store in a covered jar.

> Suddenly he began speaking to the fish in
> their illuminated tanks. "Now at last I can
> look at you in peace, I don't eat you
> anymore."
>
> MAX BROD, recounting a story
> about Franz Kafka

China

"Bring us two bowls of noodles, a platter of salted vegetables, and a large pot of hot tea." . . . Such a request must have been heard frequently in the eating-houses of China during the course of her long history. The one quoted comes from *The Chinese Gold Murders*,* and the speaker is that most erudite of detectives, Judge Dee.

It is pleasant to sit late on a winter's night with a large bowl of soft-fried noodles, sipping fragrant jasmine tea, and talking between the mouthfuls. For soft-fried noodles can be not only satisfying and succulent but, accompanied by side-dishes like sweet-sour radishes, soy-cooked watercress and quick salted cucumbers, can achieve the elegance of a minor feast.

SOFT-FRIED NOODLES

Only the best noodles will do: width—maximum ¼ inch. A good noodle, according to one rather decadent connoisseur of the subject, should have the quality of a velvet finger stroking the palate as it goes down.

Boil ½ **lb. noodles** in lightly salted water till only *just* tender. Drain well. In a large heavy frying pan heat **2 tbs. peanut oil** (you can use other oils, but peanut oil will fry foods closest to the authentic Chinese flavour). When the oil is very hot, add a **large crushed clove of garlic** plus a slice of **fresh ginger** (which can be put through the garlic press as well) and, immediately after, the drained noodles. Stirring carefully, so that the noodles don't stick to the bottom of the pan, heat through thoroughly for about 2 minutes. Now add **1 tbs. soy sauce** and ⅛ **tsp. sea-salt** and mix in well. Serve in deep, warmed individual bowls. (3)

SWEET-SOUR RADISHES

Wash a **small bunch of firm radishes** and dry well. Make 2 or 3 fairly deep gashes in each radish and drop them into a

* By R. van Gulik—Michael Joseph, 1959.

dry glass jar—the narrower and taller the better. Prepare a marinade of the following: **2 tsp. peanut oil, 2 tbs. medium-sweet sherry, 1 tbs. demerara sugar, 4 tsp. good wine vinegar, 1 tsp. sea-salt.** Stir well till amalgamated, then pour over the radishes. Cover jar tight and refrigerate an hour before using.

QUICK SALTED CUCUMBERS

Slice firm **cucumbers** into ⅛-inch rounds, sprinkle with **sea-salt,** and let stand for a ½ hour. Drain and serve.

SOY-COOKED WATERCRESS

Carefully wash **2 or 3 bunches of watercress** and remove the tough part of the stems. Plunge the cress into a saucepan containing ½ **cup boiling salted water** (¼ **tsp. sea-salt** should be adequate), add a **bruised clove of garlic** and **2 tbs. soy sauce.** Cook gently till tender, about 15 minutes, then allow to cool. Remember to remove the bruised garlic clove before serving in the cooking juices. (2–3)

GLUTEN

Sheer necessity compelled millions of Chinese throughout the ages to adopt a mainly vegetarian diet.* Sensibility of taste and a natural curiosity, however, led them to create highly palatable dishes from even the humblest of ingredients. One of the most versatile of these is Wheat Gluten, a substance rich in protein and with a texture not very unlike that of meat. Wheat Gluten can be prepared very simply at home or bought ready made in a sauce from any health food store (meatless steaks). Gluten from China is also available in Chinese food stores or from stores carrying Chinese tinned products. There is also a Japanese variety.

To make Gluten at home: mix **1 lb. plain flour** (preferably *strong* plain flour) together with **1½ tsp. sea-salt** and enough

---

* As recently as the twenties and thirties, Chinese rickshaw men were subsisting on practically nothing but daily handfuls of rice. A team of German and Swiss doctors examined these agile human hauliers and found them not only healthy but free of gastric ulcers and high blood pressure and, most curious of all, among the most fertile of all that highly fertile people. The rice diet for high blood pressure is still widely practised on the Continent and in America (the *Kempner Diet*). Its value has also been proved by outstanding clinical results in the treatment and curing of the most dangerous illnesses of the heart and vascular system.

cold water—approximately 1 cup—to form a firm dough. Knead well for 4–5 minutes. Fill a deep bowl with cold water, dissolve **2–3 tbs. sea-salt** in it, put the dough in and push well below the surface. Let it remain there for ½ hour, then transfer it to a sieve or colander. With a stream of cold tap water running steadily over it, squeeze the dough between your fingers until all the starch has been washed away. You will notice an interesting change taking place; from being gummy and a little hard to handle at first, the ball of dough will gradually amalgamate itself into a tight elastic whole. This is your Gluten. Continue the squeezing process till the water runs clear instead of milky.

Let the Gluten stand on a plate for about 15 minutes, when it will have expelled most of its surplus water. Then place it in the bottom of a suitable wire steamer. Steam for 15 minutes over rapidly boiling **vegetable stock** (made up from **Instant Soup mix**), enriched with a generous splash of **soy sauce** and a **garlic clove** cut in half. Steam for 30 minutes if you are using *strong* flour Gluten and turn the piece over once—half-way through. Cool, then store in a covered container in the refrigerator till needed. (A dough made up from 1 lb. strong flour will produce about 8 oz. of gluten.)

BREADED GLUTEN SWEET AND SOUR

Slice **8 oz. gluten**—home-prepared variety—into pieces approximately 1 inch wide, 2 inches long.

Break a **large egg** into a bowl, beat well, add ¾ **tsp. soy sauce** and a **small crushed clove of garlic.** Have a good supply of **very fine bread-crumbs** ready.

Heat **2–3 tbs. peanut oil** in a large heavy pan and, when hot, arrange in the gluten pieces which have been first egg-dipped and rolled in the crumbs. Fry till both surfaces are really crisp and golden, then drain on brown paper.

For the sweet-sour sauce: stir together ½ **cup wine vinegar,** ½ **cup demerara sugar, 2 tsp. soy sauce,** a fine chopped slice of **fresh ginger, 2 tsp. diced pimento,** ½ **tsp. sea-salt,** ¼ **tsp. corn flour.** Fry a **crushed clove of garlic** in a well-oiled pan for a few minutes then follow with the liquid mixture. Bring to a slow simmer, add several twists of **lemon rind,** and continue heating gently for 4–5 minutes.

Cut the breaded gluten into ½-inch wide slices, put in with the sweet-sour sauce and heat through quickly. Serve with bowls of **dry-cooked rice** (see below), topped by slivers of **spring onion** cut lengthwise. (2–3)

BREADED GLUTEN PINEAPPLE

Exactly as before, only, for the sauce, reduce the amount of sugar by half and add **3–4 tbs. diced tinned pineapple** and a **¼ cup of the pineapple liquid.**

COLD BREADED GLUTEN

Prepare a sufficient quantity of **breaded gluten** and allow to cool. Arrange on a long platter and sprinkle liberally with **toasted crushed almonds** and slivers of **spring onion** cut lengthwise. Serve together with individual small bowls of **soy sauce** for frequent dipping while eating.

FRIED-STIRRED VEGETABLES

The city of Hankow in thirteenth century China was renowned for many things not least for the variety and quantity of fruit and vegetable produce which streamed into its markets. There were eighteen different types of haricots, nine of rice, eleven of apricots, eight of pears. In fact, there was hardly a species of growing thing which did not have some variant of its kind. In a land where only the rich were accustomed to the taste of meat, the preparation of vegetables became almost an art. We owe the quick-fry method of cookery to Chinese inventiveness, a method which leaves vegetables subtly crisp and juicy, while most of their goodness remains unimpaired.

Practically any vegetable can be used this way—watercress, bean sprouts, celery, cabbage, mushrooms, cauliflower, aubergines, batavia, cucumber, pumpkin. The only limitation is availability. Whichever vegetables you use, however, should be well washed and/or prepared in the following way:

watercress—the thick stems discarded
bean sprouts—just rinsed in cold water
celery—sliced thin on the diagonal
cabbage—thinly shredded
mushrooms—peeled and cut into fair-sized chunks
cauliflower—the flowerets sliced thin, the green stems cut diagonally and very fine
aubergines—cut in 1-inch cubes, salted, left to stand in a sieve for an hour under a weight, then rinsed and dried
batavia—the leaves cut in rather large pieces

cucumber—peeled and sliced in thin diagonal rounds
pumpkin—peeled, the seeds and pith removed, the flesh cut
into small squares about ⅛ inch thick.

Chinese meals usually consist of a variety of dishes at a time.
It is therefore a good idea to make the selection as interesting as
possible, say a dish of fried-stirred cabbage with one of mushrooms, one of bean sprouts, and one of watercress or celery.

Prepare the vegetables of your choice as above (**1½ cups of
each),** and set them out in separate mounds on your working
surface, together with a quantity of **chopped onion,** fine
sliced strips of **fresh ginger,** peeled **garlic cloves,** a ½ **cup
water** in which ½ **tsp. cornflour** has been melted. After each
vegetable has been fried, turn it into an *individual* bowl and
keep it very warm. The time taken for quick-frying all the
vegetables should occupy you for no more than minutes.

In a heavy frying pan heat **4 tsp. peanut oil.** Before it
becomes too hot add a crushed garlic clove, 2-3 tbs. chopped
onion, some strips of ginger. Stir—and just as the onion is
beginning to mellow add 1½ cups of prepared vegetable. Raise
to a brisk heat. Keep the vegetable pieces moving in the pan
with a fork continuously for about 2-3 minutes, then add **2 tsp.
soy sauce** and a sprinkle of **sea-salt** and continue the process
for another 2-3 minutes (*this is the quick-fry method*). By this
time the bottom of the pan should be quite tacky. Pour in
2 tbs. of the cornflour water, scrape the bottom of the pan so
that a rich gravy froths up. Cook briskly another minute only.
Turn pan contents into a bowl and keep very warm. Repeat
procedure with 1½ cups of the next vegetable—until all the
vegetables have been quick-fried. Serve topped with a few
crushed toasted almonds, accompany with **soft-fried
noodles** or **dry-cooked rice,** and medium-dry sherry—
preferably very cold. (Four quick-fried dishes with rice or
noodles should serve 3-4.)

VEGETABLE CHOP SUEY

A more elaborate presentation of the quick-fry method where
several vegetables are cooked and served in combination. A
good selection would be ½ **lb. fresh bean sprouts,** ¼ **lb.
button mushrooms, 2 stalks celery,** 1½ **tbs. chopped
green or red pepper** (sweet), **3 tbs. chopped onion, 1 garlic
clove,** a good slice of **fresh ginger** in fine strips.

Prepare vegetables in the suggested manner.

Heat 1½ **tbs. peanut oil** in pan, add the onion, ginger and crushed garlic. As the onion begins to mellow add the chunks of mushroom, together with **1 tsp. soy sauce,** and quick-fry on a brisk heat for 2–3 minutes. Remove mushrooms and onion to a warm bowl, add celery and sweet pepper to the pan, and a little more oil if necessary. Quick-fry for 2–3 minutes, then add the bean sprouts and an additional tbs. of soy sauce. Quick-fry again. Pour in ¼ **cup cold water** in which ¼ **tsp. cornflour** has been dissolved. Scrape the bottom of the pan. Return the mushrooms and onion to the pan and stir through thoroughly for a minute longer. Serve immediately on hot platters, accompany with dry-cooked rice. (Serves 3)

DRY-COOKED RICE

Rich is the year with much millet and rice,
And we have tall granaries
With hundreds and thousands and millions of sheaves.
We make wine and sweet spirits
To offer to ancestor and ancestress,
Thus to fulfil all the rites
And bring down blessings in full.

Book of the Odes (*Shih ching*) c. 600 B.C.

One of the delights of any Chinese meal is the perfectly dry, fluffy white rice with which it is accompanied. Each grain should have a singleness from its neighbour, yet a light clingingness when pressed together, and a delicate, almost nut-like flavour.

To **each cup of patna (long-grain) rice**—well rinsed in five or six changes of water, then drained—allow just a little over a cup of cold water. Say, 1¼ **cups cold water**—ample for American patna style rice, not always enough for Asian rices which can be older, and dryer. It is advisable to find a rice whose taste you like, then stick with it more or less till you get to know its characteristics.

Put the rice and water in a heavy saucepan, bring to the boil, turn heat down immediately and cover. Continue to cook very gently for approximately 10 minutes. By this time most or all the water should have been absorbed. Test the rice by tasting it. If it is nearly, *nearly nearly*, done, remove the saucepan, covered again, to the side of the cooker and keep it warm. Let it steam there, another 20–30 minutes at least—or for the length of time it takes you to make up the rest of the meal. Take cover off occasionally and shake away the condensed water. Now when you taste it you should find it cooked completely—dry texture, grain separate, nut-like flavour.

Is it nowhere completely done (that is, after the 10 minutes)? Then add another ⅛ to ¼ cup water, but try not to overdo it, and keep a record of the water proportions. Continue to cook gently another 3–4 minutes. Now test it, and decide whether it is ready either for steaming, or for a few drops more water.

If you have any rice left over from your meal, put it into a covered container in the refrigerator. It is delicious fried up next day in a little **peanut oil,** together with chopped **sweet onion, bean sprouts, celery, soy sauce** and any other savoury ingredient you fancy.

The legendary emperors Yao and Shun were admired for their lives of virtuous simplicity. They were said to have eaten and drunk from unglazed earthen bowls and their food was coarse grain with a soup of greens.

Soups containing greens of one sort or another have always been considered refreshing and invigorating by the Chinese. For the rather exquisite concoction which follows, it will be best to use the Instant Soup mix.

GREENS AND EGG-FROTH SOUP

To each cup of water allow **1–1¼ tsp. Instant Soup powder.** Bring water to the boil and add the soup mix. In the meantime, beat an **egg** (1 egg for 2–3 servings, 2 eggs for 3–5) very well together with ¼ **tsp. cornflour.**

For the greens, **watercress** is best, although fine sliced young **green beans, pois mange tout, batavia, shredded lettuce** or **spinach** will do.

Pour the egg mixture through a sieve, little by little, into the boiling soup. Turn down heat and simmer for 1 minute. Now toss in some well-washed greens plus a thin slice of **fresh ginger** and cook gently for no more than a further minute—it is important to keep the vegetable as crisp as possible, so that its texture presents a distinct contrast to the velvety texture of the egg.

Serve in individual Chinese bowls. Season with a little **soy sauce.**

WHITE MUSHROOM AND GINGER SOUP

Bring 1½ **pints water** to the boil in a saucepan. Flavour with

3-3¾ **tsp. Instant Soup mix.** Stir well, then add ¼ **lb. perfectly white button mushrooms,** sliced very thin, together with a thin slice of **ginger** (about $\frac{1}{16}$ inch thick). Simmer 2-3 minutes only. Serve immediately. Season with a little **soy sauce.** (3)

AT-ONCE-SOUP

Rub each soup bowl with a cut clove of **garlic,** then add: ⅛ **tsp. vegetable shmaltz** (p. 150), ⅛ **tsp. sea-salt, 1 tsp. soy sauce, 1 tbs. top leaves of watercress,** a sliver of **fresh ginger, 1 tsp. chopped spring onion.** When ready to serve, merely add **boiling water** to each bowl and stir well.

A light and digestible accompaniment to fried-stirred vegetables or breaded gluten.

MUSHROOM FRIED ALMONDS

Blanch **1 oz. almonds,** remove skins, split each into half. Fry to pale golden in **2 tbs. peanut oil,** tilting the pan if necessary to ensure a sufficient depth of oil. This requires careful attention as the almonds tend to burn easily if left too long or if the oil is overly hot and smoking. Remove almonds and drain on brown paper. Leave the remaining oil in the pan.

Cut **6 oz. firm button mushrooms** into thick chunks.

Over a medium heat fry **2 tbs. chopped sweet onion.** When translucent, add the mushrooms and quick-fry for 2 minutes. Now add **1 tbs. soy sauce** and continue stirring so that the mushrooms become thoroughly glazed. As the bottom of the pan becomes brown and tacky add in **2 tbs. cold water** and cook for another minute only. Remove from heat and transfer mushrooms, onion and cooking juices to a warm bowl. Top with the fried almonds and slivers of length-cut **spring onion.** (2)

Serve with Egg Rolls.

EGG ROLLS

Prepare a quantity of **pancakes** (p. 27), about 6 inches in diameter, griddle-baked on one side only. Spread the middles of the baked sides with a combination of the following: **bean sprouts, chopped sweet pepper, chopped sweet onion, chopped celery,** a fine mincing of **fresh ginger.**

Roll up into cylinder-shaped envelopes—by first rolling up over the filling, tucking in both sides, then rolling up completely. Brush edges with the **white of an egg.** Drop carefully into medium hot **deep oil** and fry till rich golden. Drain. Dip as you eat into soy sauce.

PLUM SAUCE

This fruity relish is delightful with all fried-stirred vegetable dishes or cold breaded gluten.

Combine **1 cup plum jam,** not too sweet, with ½ **cup hot chutney, 2 tsp. demerara sugar, 2 tsp. red wine vinegar, 1 tbs. chopped sweet red pepper,** and a sliver of **crushed garlic.** Let it stand for at least 2 hours in a cold place before using. It will taste even better after several days maturing.

> The human-hearted man, in regard to animals, having seen them ... receptive to the warmth of the sun and the companionships of their own kind, prefers to partake of foods which do not derive from these lesser brethren of his.
>
> MENCIUS

Japan

Shirodayu: No need for anything fancy.
There's some rice left over from this
morning. I boiled some seaweed so we
won't have to waste time on that. The
radishes are right over there . . .

from *The House of Sugawara*
18th century Doll Theatre play

No need for anything fancy . . . because the character who is
speaking just can't be bothered. But even in the most fastidious
of Japanese households the accent is still on simple ingredients—
prepared with artistry.

There is a stylization about Japanese food preparation which,
at its best, is as formal as the tea-making ceremony. The use of
special plates and bowls, of distinctive or plain pattern, the
arrangement of ingredients into contrasting or complementary
colours, the essential simplicity of the fare—all these combine to
make the Japanese way of eating an eye-appealing as well as a
purely sensuous pleasure.

SEAWEED SUKIYAKI

Prepare

1 cup white cabbage—fine-shredded
½ **cup cauliflower**—fine-sliced
½ **cup young string beans**—sliced diagonally and thin
1 celery stalk—cut in thin diagonal sections
1 medium size carrot—in thin diagonal rounds

Cook a square of *Konbu* **seaweed** (see p. 17) in a small
saucepan of water. Cook till soft, then drain, cool and cut into
small squares.

Heat **1 tbs. peanut oil** in a large heavy pan and, when very
hot, toss in **2 chopped spring onions, 1 tsp. mustard seed**
(black), **2 thin slices of fresh ginger,** a crushed clove of
garlic. Let cook fiercely a moment or two, then add the
prepared vegetables, 1½ **tbs. soy sauce** (Kikkoman for

preference*), a sprinkling of **sea-salt.** Reduce heat, stir through, cook gently for 5 minutes, stirring frequently. Now add the diced *Konbu* and ¼ **cup cold water.** Raise heat briefly, then reduce, simmer another 2–3 minutes only.

Serve immediately with **dry-cooked rice** (p. 89), **pickled side-dishes** or chilled **green salad.** (Enough for 2–3)

Variation: Make up a Sukiyaki sauce: 1½ **tsp. sesame oil, 2 tsp. very dry red wine, 1 tsp. corn flour, 1½ tsp. sea-salt, 4 tbs. saké** (or **dry sherry**), **1 tsp. demerara sugar, 1 tbs. water.** Heat together in a small saucepan for 2–3 minutes. Stir well. Keep warm.

Now proceed as before but omit the seaweed. After the onion, mustard seed, ginger and garlic have been fried, add the prepared vegetables—minus the soy sauce and sea-salt—cook gently for 5 minutes, stirring frequently. Now add the Sukiyaki sauce, and simmer till it thickens.

PICKLED LETTUCE AND CUCUMBER

Cut a very fresh **cos lettuce** down the centre. Rinse well and shake out thoroughly. Place in a deep bowl, cut side up, sprinkle liberally with **sea-salt.**

Peel and slice a large, firm **cucumber** into ¼-inch-thick diagonal rounds. Arrange over the lettuce. Sprinkle liberally with sea-salt.

Store in a cool place for 2 days. Serve as an accompaniment to Seaweed Sukiyaki, or as a separate course with other side-dishes and rice.

PICKLED MELON

Cut the flesh of a sweet **melon** into thick chunks. Place in a small deep bowl, immerse in **saké** (if available), otherwise in **dry sherry.** Add a light sprinkling of **sea-salt.** Allow to marinate 4–5 days before using.

MUSHROOM WATERCRESS SOUP

Wash **2 bunches watercress,** shake dry, remove thick stalks. Then chop coarsely. Cut **2 oz. white button mushrooms** into fairly thin slices. Cut **2 or 3 spring onions** into ½-inch lengths.

Heat **2 tsp. peanut oil** in a saucepan, add the cut onion and

---

* Kikkoman is to be preferred in the preparation of Japanese dishes.

fry gently a few minutes. Then follow with the watercress and **3½ cups cold water.** Bring to the boil, reduce heat, add the mushrooms. Simmer 5 minutes. Just before removing from heat add **1½ tbs. soy sauce** and a light sprinkling of **sea-salt.** Stir through. (Serves 4)

SESAME SAUCE

Delicious with all rice and vegetable dishes.

Lightly toast ¼ **cup sesame seeds** under the grill. When cool, pulverize in a mortar. Add **2 tbs. demerara sugar, 2 tbs. soy sauce, 2 tbs. wine vinegar,** and amalgamate thoroughly.

For more extended use make up the same ingredients in proportionally larger amounts, bottle and store in the refrigerator.

VEGETABLES TEMPURA

Choose vegetables like **cauliflower, young green beans, onion, celery, courgettes**—about 1 lb. altogether. Cut into smallish pieces, then parboil for 5–7 minutes. Drain.

Make up a sauce of the following: ½ **cup Instant Soup stock** (suggested addition of soup powder: ¾ tsp.), **2 tbs. saké** or **dry sherry, 2 tbs. soy sauce,** a small piece of **fresh ginger,** bruised. Bring to the boil in a small saucepan, simmer 5 minutes, strain, let get completely cold.

Heat a saucepan of **peanut oil** for deep frying.

Make up a tempura batter: mix together lightly **1 cup plain flour** with **4 eggs,** ¼ **cup cold water,** a small crushed **garlic clove** (optional). Dip vegetable pieces into batter and fry till crisp and golden. Drain well, then pierce assortments of the vegetables on to individual wooden skewers. Serve over beds of **dry-cooked rice.** Accompany with the tempura sauce in bowls suitable for dipping. (4–6)

BAMBOO SHOOTS AND MUSHROOMS

Prepare

½ **cup tinned bamboo shoots**—cut in thin diagonal slices
1 cup mushrooms—in thick chunks
¼ **cup young green beans**—cut into lengthwise strips
½ **cup sweet onion**—in thin rings
1 celery stalk—in ¼-inch diagonal sections

In a small saucepan simmer **2 tbs. soy sauce,** ½ **cup Instant Soup stock** (see sauce for Vegetables Tempura above), **1**

small crushed clove of garlic, 1 tbs. mild honey. Simmer
3 minutes, stir through, remove from heat, keep warm.

Heat 1½ **tbs. peanut oil** in a large heavy pan. Add the
onions and brown lightly. Follow with the rest of the vegetables,
cook briskly for 2–3 minutes, stirring and turning frequently.

Now add half the sauce, reduce heat, simmer 5 minutes.
Now the rest of the sauce, and heat through thoroughly.

Serve over **dry-cooked rice,** top with **toasted almond
halves.** (2–3)

> The radish picker
> with his radish
> points the way
>
> KOBAYASHI ISSA (18th–19th cent.)

The radish picker in Kobayashi's *haiku* was undoubtedly giving
directions to a traveller, probably Kobayashi himself. But in
another manner of speaking he has always been pointing the
way. For the radish, like the potato in the west, has traditionally
played a basic and varied role in the national diet ... Pickled,
fried or raw. Grated and salted as an instant relish. Sliced and
added to soups for flavouring. Crushed and marinated in soy
sauce and saké as a quick pickle to accompany rice and noodle
dishes.

The following recipe employs *white raddish*, sometimes con-
fusingly known as *black raddish* because of its outer skin colouring, but the flesh is pure white.

RAINBOW SALAD

Prepare ½ **cup each of white (black) radish, carrot,** and
cucumber, as follows:

Peel and cut radish and carrot into very thin longitudinal
strips. Place each vegetable in separate bowls.

Wash cucumber but do not peel. Cut into half crosswise, then
lengthwise, remove seeds. Then cut into strips, as before, and
place in a separate bowl. (Radish and cucumber strips should
roughly correspond in length with carrot strips.)

Sprinkle contents of each bowl lightly with **sea-salt** and
wine vinegar and allow to stand till somewhat softened—
about 10–15 minutes. Then drain and press out the liquid from
each of the bowls. Place all the cut vegetables in a large salad
bowl.

Cut **2 oz. button mushrooms** into fine strips, add to the

ingredients in the salad bowl. Sprinkle over with **2 tsp. wine vinegar.**

Beat **2 eggs** together, add **2 tsp. demerara sugar,** a rounded ½ **tsp. sea-salt.** Beat again. Fry in a small heavy pan in **1 tsp. peanut oil,** stirring constantly, till a granular mixture forms. Turn out immediately into a sieve, press the mixture through, allow to cool. Blend with **2 tsp. wine vinegar.**

When ready to serve, combine the egg mixture with the contents of the salad bowl—very thoroughly—mixing and distributing the colours well. Top with **crushed toasted almonds** and slivers of **spring onion.** (4–5)

VEGETABLE ROUND CAKES

Beat **4 eggs** together, add to a mixture of the following:

¼ **cup water chestnuts**—sliced fine
½ **cup fresh bean sprouts**
1 **celery stalk**—sliced fine
1 **tbs. chopped sweet onion**
2 **tsp. chopped sweet red pepper**

Blend thoroughly, mix with enough **matzo meal** to form a light batter.

Heat a shallow depth of **peanut oil** in a heavy pan. When hot, drop batter in by spoonfuls. Fry till both sides are crisp and brown. Drain. Serve with small bowls of **soy sauce** for dipping. Accompany with Pickled Melon or Pickled Lettuce and Cucumber. (4)

GOMA SIO

A very flavoursome condiment to sprinkle over rice, fried vegetables, and many other savoury dishes, an excellent alternative to salt.

Lightly toast ¼ **cup sesame seeds** under the grill. Cool. Put in a mortar along with **1½ tsp. sea-salt.** Pound and grind very thoroughly. Store in an air-tight container, or in a restaurant-style glass sugar dispenser. Use liberally.

GREEN BEANS STEAMED EGGS

Trim the ends of **4 oz. young green beans,** cut into ½-inch sections.

Dissolve **1 tbs. demerara sugar** in a solution of **2 tbs. soy sauce/2 tbs. water.** Add **1 tsp. fine minced onion.** Pour the mixture into a heavy pan, set on a low heat, arrange in the green bean sections, simmer till almost tender (10–12 minutes).

Remove **1 tbs. liquid** from the pan and discard. Beat **4 eggs** together very well, pour over the green beans, cover pan, steam gently 4–5 minutes, or till eggs are set and nicely puffed. (Serves 2–3)

Accompany with Red-Cooked Mushroom.

RED-COOKED MUSHROOM

Use 4 oz. of the largest **mushrooms** you can get. Clean with a damp cloth, or peel, trim stalks short. Stand caps in a mixture of **3 tbs. soy sauce, 1 tbs. dry sherry, 2 tbs. peanut oil, 2 tsp. honey, 1 crushed garlic clove.** Allow to stand 10–15 minutes.

Arrange mushrooms, cap sides up, in a shallow baking pan, and grill under a medium heat till brown, warm reddish-brown, in fact. Turn stalk sides up and grill a further 3–4 minutes. (Serves 2)

India

... an elephant as tall as a tree and
gentle as the motherly Cow ... led Duryodhana and his retinue safely from the
jungle.

The Miraculous Monkey

Poor Prince Duryodhana ... not only is he unsuccessful in his
attempts to capture the sacred talking monkey, but that baleful
animal continues to flit through the trees above him and his
party, taunting them with outrageous remarks. And then Duryodhana is exposed to the sight of a lavish display of all his
favourite dishes, each wafting to his nostrils the most intoxicating of aromas. His elderly, and by this time weary, adviser
assures him that it is only a product of enchantment, which
opinion Duryodhana characteristically and hot-headedly
ignores. He dashes forward and is just on the point of falling on
the food when he knocks his brow against a barely visible
crystal door—another product of enchantment! And now the
door, together with the banquet, conveniently disappear.
"Duryodhana's head ached and his brains reeled and his
followers, dismayed, stood about ..." And, no doubt, the
sacred talking monkey just laughed and laughed.

Poor Prince Duryodhana ... even if we are not on the quest
of sacred talking monkeys (nowadays there seem to be other
problems), we can still sympathize with him. Some of us, at one
time or other, have bumped our heads into glass (crystal) doors
which didn't seem to be there. Others, though not ardent
gluttons like him, can certainly understand his feelings when we
happen to pass some Indian restaurant and those highly
enticing aromas are wafted out.

To produce similar aromas in our own kitchens, and the
innumerable nuances of delicious flavour that go along with
them, let us first consider spices.

Spices and herbs in Indian cookery are usually used in
particular combinations. Sometimes this is with the addition

of curry powder, most often it is without. Indian spices and herbs range from the pungent and hot to the very aromatic and mild. It is advisable to set up a small store of them. The expense is very modest, as most of them can be bought by the ounce. Spices and herbs are sold and used in both seed and powdered form. Here are some of the more essential, along with a few other constituents of the Indian larder.

Cardamom   The "seed of paradise". Subtly sweet and complex flavour. Used in milk dishes, palaos, curries. Buy both seed and powder.

Chilli peppers   Both red and green chilli peppers contribute to the "hotness" of Indian dishes, and can be used as lavishly or sparingly as desired. They can even be omitted altogether, without detracting from the basic deliciousness of the food. If fresh chillies are unobtainable, substitute with dry chillies or chilli powder.

Coconut milk   Usually added toward the end of cooking to give one of those "innumerable nuances of flavour". Easily prepared from "Creamed Coconut", which comes packed in ½ lb. slabs like butter or margarine. Soak 1 tbs. "Creamed Coconut" in enough hot water to melt it—about 2 tbs. water—then stir well.

Coriander   An old friend (see p. 13). Buy both seed and powder.

Cummin   Delightfully aromatic and flavoursome—also one of the basic elements of curry powder. Buy both seed and powder.

Curry powder   A mixture of spices and herbs, roasted and pulverized. Preferable to buy the more expensive varieties since they contain additionally choice ingredients. Available either "hot" or "mild".

Garam masala   Another ready-mixed powdered condiment, usually prepared from the ground seeds of cardamom, cinnamon, cloves, mace and nutmeg. Gives a certain kind of piquancy "in depth"—added toward the end of cooking.

Ghee   What peanut oil is to Chinese cookery, ghee is to Indian. A form of clarified butter or margarine (vegetable ghee). Ordinary margarine or oil may be substituted, but at the cost of authenticity of taste. Available in tins in Indian and Greek provision stores. But if you wish to make your own, very gently melt 1 lb. of butter (or margarine) over a low heat. Stir carefully when it begins to simmer and continue stirring, till all the sediment has drifted downwards. Remove pot from heat, strain liquid through butter muslin, cool, then store in the refrigerator.

Gram flour A flour milled from *gram* (whole dried pulse), very adhesive in texture. It takes the place of eggs for binding purposes in Indian cookery.

Methe The Indian term for fenugreek. Buy seeds for preference.

Mustard seed Both the tiny white and black seeds are available. The black are more useful.

Tamarind Loose term for the pod of the tamarind tree. Unrecognizable as a pod, however, since it arrives in this country in a mashed, bulked state, somewhat straggly looking and rather sticky. Tamarind-water is added toward the end of a curry, intensifying the colour and taking some of the edge off the 'heat'. Soak a small lump (about 1 tbs.) of tamarind in enough hot water to cover for about 10 minutes, strain the liquid through butter muslin and set aside (the water, that is—the mash may be discarded). Lemon or lime juice may occasionally be substituted.

Turmeric Gives the characteristic orange-brown or golden colouring to curry dishes. Sometimes, also, the same characteristic and hard-to-remove colouring you see on tablecloths and napkins in Indian restaurants. Not surprisingly, since it has been used both as dyestuff and condiment since ancient times. Buy powder and use carefully. If you are in the habit of spilling things, however, omit entirely.

Harvest festivals are one of the oldest forms of organized jollity among agricultural peoples. With certain Hindu sects in southern India, however, the light-hearted preliminaries used to be followed by a more serious rite. On a day chosen to be fortunate by the local astrologer, each family put on a pot of the new rice to boil. The proceedings were then watched with much anxiety, for as the pot boiled so would the coming year turn out. If the boiling was fast, the year would be prosperous; but if slow, then just the opposite.

The vagaries of the yearly rice crop have always been a cause for momentous concern among eastern peoples, for it, more than any other food, provides the needs of daily nourishment. A generous portion of rice almost always accompanies Indian meals, usually with a dish of dal, chapattis, and a variety of chutneys and other relishes.

PLAIN BOILED RICE *See* Dry-Cooked Rice—China, p. 89.

FRIED RICE (I)

Wash 1¼ **cups patna rice** in 5 or 6 changes of water. Drain.

Melt **2 tbs. ghee** in a heavy frying pan, add the rice and stir —over a medium heat—till it turns pale golden. Follow with 1¾–2 **cups boiling water,** gradually, and salt to taste (about 1½ **tsp. sea-salt**). Cover pan, reduce heat, and simmer very slowly till the rice is dry and flaky. Steam on the side of the cooker for 15–20 minutes more. (Serves 4)

FRIED RICE (II)

Use **4 cups cooked patna rice** (from about 1½ cups raw). Preferably rice which has been cooked several hours beforehand, or on the previous day.

Heat **2 tbs. ghee** in a heavy pan. Add ¼ **tsp. powdered cinnamon,** ¼ **tsp. cummin seed, 2 whole cloves, 3 tbs. chopped onion.** Fry on a medium heat till onion turns light brown. Stir in the rice, amalgamate thoroughly, and continue frying (and stirring) till the rice is heated through—about 5 minutes. (4–6)

COCONUT RICE (South India)

A rather more sumptuous way of preparation.

Wash 1¼ **cups patna rice** in several changes of water, drain, set to soak in fresh water for 1 hour. Drain again, very well.

Melt **2 tbs. ghee** in a large heavy pan, add **a small diced onion** and fry gently for 5 minutes. Now add the rice, stir through thoroughly, and 1½ cups liquid prepared as follows: put **6 tbs. "Creamed Coconut"** in a one pint measuring cup; add enough **hot water** to dissolve it, then bring the liquid level up to 1½ cups. Blend coconut milk and rice, add **1 tsp. sea-salt,** cover pan and simmer gently till liquid absorbs. Then steam on the side of the cooker 15–20 minutes more. Serve hot. (4)

VEGETABLE PALAO

Another sumptuous one, but in quite a different manner— decorative to the eye, light and pleasing to the palate, a more complete meal in itself with its integration of vegetables.

Wash 1¾ **cups patna rice** in the usual way, drain, and set to cook in a little less than 2¼ **cups water**—dry-cooked method (p. 89). Add a small pinch of **saffron powder** to the cooking water. A pinch only, which will colour the rice a lovely golden-yellow without giving it a saffron taste.

Meantime, roast and crush **2 oz. pistachios** (or **almonds, if you don't have any pistachios**).

Over a low heat, in **2 tbs. ghee,** fry a **small onion** cut into rings. Fry till light brown. Remove onion from pan and keep warm.

Into the pan now add: **3 cardamom seeds, 1 tsp. garam masala, 1 fine chopped slice of fresh ginger, ¾ tsp. cummin seed.** Fry lightly for 3–4 minutes. Follow with the saffron rice, stir through, fry a few minutes longer. Then with ½ **cup boiled young peas,** and an assortment of any other cooked vegetables you have on hand (say a ½ cup more). Stir again and continue frying over the same slow heat till everything is heated through. Transfer contents of the pan to a well-warmed, oval-shaped bowl and serve, topped with the browned onion rings and the toasted pistachios (almonds).

If you like, you can also decorate your palao with quarters of **firm tomato,** sliced **hard-boiled egg,** chopped **spring onion** or **coriander leaves.** (Serves 6)

VEGETABLE COOKERY

A few general pointers.

Indian cooking almost always proceeds on a very, very slow heat.

Little or no water is added to the vegetables, at least at the outset—they are allowed to stew in their own juices. If water has to be added, it should be kept to a minimum. And if gravy is wanted then the water comes in only after the vegetables are more than half done.

Vegetables are cooked either singly or in combination. In the case of combinations of vegetables, those which take longest to cook are added first, those most quickly cooked, last.

DRY MIXED-VEGETABLE CURRIES

Some good mixtures would be **potatoes, carrots, cauliflower; tomatoes, green beans, potatoes; aubergines, tomatoes, sweet green peppers; yams, peas, courgettes.**

For **2 lb. vegetables,** cut into medium-sized pieces:

(1) Heat **2–3 tbs. ghee** in a large heavy pan. Fry **1 sliced medium-size onion** till translucent.

(2) Add herbs and spices: **1–2 tsp. curry powder, ¼ tsp.**

chilli powder, a generous slice of **fresh ginger** chopped fine, **4 crushed garlic cloves,** ½ tsp. **cummin seed,** a small chopped seeded **green chilli pepper** (optional). Stir through and fry lightly 3–4 minutes.

(3) Add the cut vegetables, together with **sea-salt** to taste. Stir and toss well with the other ingredients in the pan, cover, cook *very* slowly. Add a little water, only if necessary, from time to time. Stir occasionally. Cook till vegetables are very tender.

If gravy is required **water** or **coconut milk** or **buttermilk** (a few tbs. only) or fine-chopped and peeled **tomato** can be added after the half-way mark. Very often, when the vegetables are almost cooked, a small amount of **garam masala** is sprinkled in. (Serves 4–6)

QUICK MIXED-VEGETABLE CURRIES

Entirely as above, only parboil your vegetables before adding them to the onion, herbs and spices. They will then require only a further ten minutes or so in which to absorb the flavours and be cooked to completion.

PUNJABI VEGETABLE CURRY

Prepare **1 lb. peeled, diced potato;** ½ **lb. diced flowerets of cauliflower.** Have ready ½ **cup young green peas.**

Heat **2–3 tbs. ghee** in a large heavy pan and fry **1 sliced medium size onion** in it for 3–4 minutes—slowly. Sprinkle in **1 tsp. coriander seed,** ¾ **tsp. cummin seed, 1 chopped (seeded) green chilli pepper,** ⅛ **tsp. chilli powder, 1 crushed garlic clove.** Mix through and fry for 3 minutes longer, then add the vegetables—all at once in this particular case, since we are going to cook them till they are nearly falling apart. Stir once more, add a sprinkling of **sea-salt,** cover the pan. Add dashes of water from time to time to encourage the falling-apart process. Very near the end, add **2 tbs. coconut milk,** shake the pan to distribute the liquid, complete cooking below the simmering point—a minute or two longer. (4)

BRINJAL FOOGATH

Wash **2 medium size aubergines (12 oz.),** leave peel on. Cut into ⅛-inch-thick slices lengthwise. Salt liberally, put in a sieve under a weight for an hour, rub off salt and pat dry.

Melt **2 tbs. ghee** in a heavy pan. Raise to a brisk heat. Fry the aubergine slices, a few at a time, till both sides are golden. Remove aubergine slices to a plate as they are done. Add extra ghee to the pan from time to time.

Reduce heat to low, add a little more ghee to the pan, follow with ¼ **tsp. mustard seed,** ¼ **tsp. crushed coriander seed,** ¼ **tsp. cummin seed,** ¼ **tsp. chilli powder.** Fry a minute or so, then arrange in the aubergine slices. Now pour in ¾ **cup buttermilk** in which **1 tsp. sea-salt** and **2 crushed cloves of garlic** have been mixed. Shake pan to distribute, cover, cook very slowly for ½ hour. (4–6)

VEGETABLE MARROW CHAKEE

Remove peel, seeds and pith from **1½ lb. vegetable marrow.** Grate fine. Squeeze out most of the liquid and place the grated marrow in a bowl. Mix together with **1–2 chopped, seeded green chillies, 1½ tbs. fresh coriander leaves, 1 small crushed clove of garlic, 1 tsp. garam masala, sea-salt,** and just enough **gram flour** to bind everything together. Form into small balls and deep-fry till brown and crisp. Drain and set aside.

Heat **1½ tbs. ghee** in a heavy pan. Add **2 tsp. coriander seed,** ½ **tsp. turmeric,** ¼ **tsp. chilli powder,** ½ **tsp. cummin powder.** Fry gently for 5 minutes. Now stir in **4 medium size, fine-chopped, peeled tomatoes** plus ½ **cup hot water** and continue cooking gently for a further 10 minutes. Now add the marrow balls, cover the pan, and simmer till the gravy thickens. (4)

POTATO BONDA

The potato, that ubiquitous tuber, haunts Indian cookery just as much as our own.

Boil ½ **lb. potatoes** till tender, cool, peel, mash smooth. Add ½ **tsp. sea-salt,** a **small onion** finely chopped, a few chopped **coriander leaves,** a sprinkling of **chilli powder.** Blend together well, then form into balls the size of small plums.

Put ½ **cup gram flour** into a bowl. Add **1 tsp. sea-salt, 1 tsp. turmeric, 5–6 tbs. water** (enough to make a fairly thick batter). Coat potato balls with the batter and deep-fry till crisp and lightly browned. Fry a few only at a time. Drain on crumpled paper. (Makes 8 *bonda*)

Serve as a pre-meal appetizer, accompanied by **yoghourt** laced with **chilli powder** and fine chopped **coriander leaves.**

POTATO BHAJI

Scrub the skins of **1½–2 lb. medium potatoes** and cut, without peeling them, into lengthwise sections a little less than ½ inch thick.

Heat **3 tbs. ghee** in a large heavy pan, sprinkle in ½ **tsp. methe seed,** then arrange in the potato sections. Cover, cook over a gentle heat. When half done—about 15–20 minutes—strew in thin cut slices of ½ **Spanish onion.** Turn potatoes over and cook further—about 5 minutes—till onion becomes softened. Now add **4 cloves crushed garlic, 1–2 seeded, chopped chilli peppers,** ¾ **tsp. turmeric, 2 tbs. lemon juice,** a sprinkling of **sea-salt.** Stir lightly, continue cooking, covered, until the potatoes assume a rich browny yellow—at least another half-hour. Drizzle over with the juice of ½ **lemon,** shake the pan, serve. (Serves 3–4)

SPONGE POTATO CURRY

Grind to a fairly fine paste in a mortar: **1 medium size minced onion, 4 crushed garlic cloves,** a generous slice of **fresh ginger** (put through the garlic press as well). Blend with ½ **tsp. turmeric.**

Peel **2 lb. small potatoes** and prick each over thoroughly with a knitting needle (no. 8?) until they are almost sponge-like.

Smear the potatoes thickly with the paste and place them in a bowl containing **2 cups milk, 1 tbs. sea-salt,** the juice of a medium size **lemon.** Leave to marinate for an hour.

Now heat **2 tbs. ghee** in a large heavy pan and fry an inch-long stick of **cinammon, 4 cardamom seeds, 6 whole cloves.** Fry for a few minutes. Add the potatoes plus the milk marinade, cover, cook gently until the juices have thickened and the potatoes are meltingly tender. (4)

PULSES

Pulses (peas and lentils) form a staple in the Indian dietary and a bewildering variety of them exist. For our purpose only three will be considered (listed below). The whole dried pulse is usually referred to as *gram*, and when it is split as *dal*. It is the *dals* we are mostly interested in.

Toor dal   a medium size split lentil, orange in colour, available both dry and oily. Buy oily for preference.

Moong dal   a fairly small, maize-coloured, split lentil.
Channa dal   a medium size, beige-coloured, split lentil.

Many-flavoured dal dishes, as already mentioned, accompany rice and vegetables to make up the complete Indian meal. They are very rich in protein—and delicious. Dal is frequently poured over rice, or chapattis are dipped in it.

SOUR DAL

Soak ½ **lb. (1 cup) channa dal** in cold water overnight—or first thing in the morning for use in the evening. Then wash in several changes of water and pick over (this mainly means remove any of the occasional small stones which may have found their way in). Drain, then bring to the boil in **2½ cups water,** flavoured with ½ **tsp. turmeric** and 1½ **tsp. sea-salt.** Simmer till each lentil is tender enough to be broken easily with a ladle (approximately 50–60 minutes). Mash lightly in the pot with a potato masher. Add **1 tbs. tamarind water (or lemon juice),** a small piece of **fresh ginger** (chopped), **1 tsp. demerara sugar.** Blend well and keep hot.

Heat **1 tbs. ghee** in a small frying pan, add **3 whole cloves** and ½ **tsp. cummin seed.** Fry lightly for several minutes. Turn ghee, cloves and cummin seed into dal and mix through. If the dal is too thick for you, add a little warm water. Thinness or thickness depends on individual taste. A little **onion** can also be fried in the ghee with the cummin seed and cloves if desired. (Serves 4)

Variation: Eliminate the soaking period by using **oily toor dal** instead (see *Rasam*, below, for washing method, then cook as above—but in **3 cups water**).

AMTI DAL (Maharashtrian)

Wash ½ **lb. (1 cup) moong dal** in several changes of cold water. Pick over, drain, bring to the boil in **3 cups water** and simmer till tender (approximately 30 minutes). Mash thoroughly.

Heat **1 tbs. ghee** in a large heavy pan and, when hot, toss in **1 tbs. chopped onion, 1 crushed garlic clove, 2 cardamom seeds,** a ½**-inch stick cinnamon.** Fry lightly for several minutes till onion becomes translucent. Then add **1 rounded tsp. curry powder** and **1 large, chopped, peeled tomato** and fry a further 3 minutes, stirring all the time.

Now pour the dal into the pan together with a sprinkling of **sea-salt** (about 2½ tsp.) and cook very gently about 10 minutes. Add a little **hot water** if it becomes too thick—it should have the consistency of rich cream. Then add **1 tbs. coconut milk** and complete cooking below the simmering point—5 minutes more. (4)

RASAM (South Indian)
The "prince" of dals.

Wash ½ **lb. (1 cup) oily toor dal** in several changes of *hot* water, then several of cold. Pick over, drain, bring to the boil in **3 cups water** to which has been added a pinch of **saffron** and **1 tsp. ghee.** When quite tender (about 35-40 minutes), mash and strain through a sieve. Return to the pot, add **1 small sliced onion, 2 whole cloves, 2 small pieces of stick cinnamon, ½ tsp. demerara sugar, 1½-2 tsp. sea-salt, ¼ lb. chopped, peeled tomatoes.** Simmer till onions are soft—about 15 minutes—put dal mixture through the sieve once more (discard cinnamon and cloves). Add **lemon juice** to taste (about 1 tbs.), mix through.

In your pan, fry another small **sliced onion** in a sufficient quantity of ghee till onion is golden brown. Pour the dal into the pan, stir through, cover, simmer till well heated. (4)

FULOURIES
A savoury snack or an accompaniment to the main meal.

Chop **1 large onion** together with a handful of **coriander leaves, 1 seeded green chilli pepper,** a small piece of **fresh ginger.** Chop till fairly fine. Then season with ¼ **tsp. garam masala** and **salt** to taste.

Blend **4 tbs. gram flour** with **2 tbs. rice flour, 1 tsp. sea-salt** and enough **water (about 4 tbs.)** to make a thick batter. Allow to stand for 30 minutes. Then add **1 tsp. baking powder** to the batter, along with the onion/spice mixture. Stir very well.

Heat some **ghee** or **oil** for deep frying. When quite hot, drop the batter in by teaspoonfuls and fry till each fuloury is a nice rich brown. (4-6)

SAMOSAS
Another savoury snack, samosas are crisp-fried dough envelopes usually stuffed with a mixture of peas, potatoes and spices. They are delicious either hot or cold.

In separate saucepans, boil ½ **lb. potatoes** and ½ **lb. green peas** till tender. When cool, peel and dice the potatoes very small.

Heat **1 tbs. ghee** in a large pan and fry **1 tbs. chopped onion** till lightly golden. Follow with **1 tsp. coriander powder,** a thin slice of **fresh ginger,** chopped, ½ **tsp. turmeric,** ½ **tsp. garam masala, 1 small chopped green chilli pepper** (seeded). Fry 3 minutes longer, then add the diced potato and peas plus **1 tsp. sea-salt.** Stir thoroughly and cook well through. Finally, add a generous squeeze of **lemon juice** and let cool.

Make a dough: Rub 1½ **oz. ghee** or **margarine** through ½ **lb. sifted** *maida* **(or plain white) flour.** Rub till well-ingrained, then add enough **water (2–2½ tbs.)** to produce a fairly firm texture. Knead very well—10–15 minutes or as long as you've got the energy to—then cover with dampened butter muslin and relax . . . by looking at some of the other chapters in this book.

Form balls the size of a large walnut and roll into very thin round *puri* shapes (see below, Indian breads), about $\frac{1}{10}$ inch thick. Cut each round in half with a sharp knife. Shape each half into a cone, stuff with the vegetable/spice mixture, press edges together well. The finished product should look something like a plump triangular pillow. If necessary, seal the edges with a little flour-and-water paste. Use the dampened muslin to cover the prepared samosas, to keep from drying out.

Heat **ghee** or **oil** for deep frying (ghee will make them flakier, oil crisper), and fry a few samosas at a time, till a mature golden colour forms. Skim out and set on crumpled brown paper. (Serves 4–5)

Accompany with individual bowls of **sliced cucumber** in **yoghourt,** dotted with **chilli powder** and **sea-salt,** a variety of **chutneys,** and **Curried Gluten.**

CURRIED GLUTEN

Wash, drain and squeeze dry the contents of a **large tin of gluten** (meatless steaks). Cut into ½-inch cubes.

Fry **1 medium size, chopped sweet onion** in 4–5 **tbs. ghee** till onion is nearly golden. Add 1½ **tsp. cummin seed, 1 tsp. black mustard seed, 1 rounded tsp. coriander powder.** Stir, then fry for 3 minutes.

Put some fine **matzo meal** (or **flour**) into a bowl. Shake the gluten cubes in it till they are all lightly coated. Then add them to the pan, blend with the spices, cover, let cook slowly for about 7 minutes. Stir occasionally.

Now add **8 tbs. water, 1 tsp. sea-salt,** stir through, re-cover the pan, cook two minutes longer.* (Serves 4)

INDIAN BREADS

One of the simplest and tastiest ways of making bread is by baking it on top of a griddle. The tradition is widespread: from the Pueblos and peoples of central America (*tortillas*), to the Bedouin and deserts of Iraq (*khubiz-tabaq*), to India (*chapattis*). Because there is no leavening agent, no "rising" period, no precise oven temperature control, the margin of error in successful baking is small. The best flour for making Indian griddle bread is a wheaten one called *atta*, available in all Indian provision stores.

CHAPATTIS

Mix ½ **lb.** *atta* **flour** with enough **water (about ½ cup)** to form a soft but not sticky dough. Shape into a ball, soak under cold water for an hour. Then knead on a well-floured board for 5–10 minutes or till completely elastic. If dough is still a little sticky, add a little more *atta*. Divide into about 12 relatively equal portions—each the size of a medium plum—form into balls, between the hands, flatten, roll out into rounds about $\frac{1}{10}$ inch (or a little less) thick. Heat a dry griddle to fairly hot. Bake each chapatti on both sides—(a) till the top dries and whitens—at which point turn it over, and (b) till brown blisters form underneath.

Stack the chapattis in a tea-towel on the side of the cooker, and keep warm till serving.

* If you can ever get jack-fruit from an Indian provision store, you may be interested to try it out in much the same way as Curried Gluten—but cut it into "chops" instead of cubes. Dr. B. M. Lal of Hyderabad City, to whom we gratefully owe the solid material in this section—most of the recipes are his, the occasional banalities our own—tells us that he once entertained a Moslem colleague to breakfast, and the basis of the meal was the said jack-fruit. As the Moslem friend ate away, very enjoyably in fact, he suddenly looked up, much perplexed, and said: "But it's meat, isn't it?" Dr. Lal, who is of course a vegetarian, merely smiled obscurely. And then, as the Moslem friend, still as perplexed, went on with his eating, a large seed popped out of the fruit, whereupon both gentlemen burst into laughter.

If you have any dough left over, oil it and put it in a polythene bag into the refrigerator. Make up chapattis next morning—as a substitute for toast—butter them and salt them.

PURIS

Deep-fried Indian bread.

Put ½ **lb.** *atta* **flour** in a bowl, combine with ½ **tsp. sea-salt.** Pour in **1 tbs. olive oil,** rub oil through flour till a very fine mixture results. Then add ½ **cup** *hot* **water,** and mix to a soft dough. Knead on a floured board till pliable—about 5 minutes. Cover dough with polythene, to prevent it drying out. Pinch off a small piece at a time—the size of a walnut—form into a ball between the hands, flatten, roll out as follows: Roll from the edges toward the middle, all round, so that the middle becomes slightly humped. Then one quick roll across the whole puri. (The outer edge should be a little more than $\frac{1}{16}$ inch thick.) Drop puris, one at a time, into deep hot **vegetable ghee.** Leave each till it billows up, wait a few moments, then turn it over. Cook till the other side is rich golden. Remove puris by tilting them up on edge with a spatula, then holding them against the side of the pot till most of the ghee runs off. Drain on absorbent paper. Serve hot.

Variation: Spiced Puris   After you have combined the flour with the **salt**—¾–**1 tsp.** this time—add small amounts of **cummin seed, chilli powder, turmeric.** Proceed as before with the oil and hot water, then roll out, straightforwardly, into thin round discs, a little thinner than before. Now, using the dull side of a knife, tap the puris all over, this way and that, crisscross, etc. (this is to *prevent* them from billowing up). Don't worry if the knife breaks the dough in places. Drop puris, one at a time, into the hot ghee, cook till both sides are golden brown.

Made this way, as a delightful crisp savoury, puris can last for several days.

CHUTNEYS, PICKLES, QUICK RELISHES

There are chutneys so mild that their fruity essences run over the palate like a stream of honey. There are equally others so spiced that they fill the head with steam and insolent pride. If you are of the *rajassic* temperament (emotional, tempestuous), you may prefer the latter. If of the *sattvic* (serene, thoughtful), the former. If you are neither, you will be content to sample the ones that fall between, and there are certainly enough to choose from ... from the delicate all the way to the tear-inducing, almost a barometer of the varying "heats" of all men. Wise India!

Besides the many excellent qualities and varieties which can be bought ready prepared in Indian provision stores—hot or mild mango chutney, lime-pickle, brinjal-pickle—you can, like the Indian housewife, improvise many more right at home. Usually three or four small dishes of chutney and relishes accompany the meal. Here are a few in the "instant" class:

(1) **Mashed boiled potatoes** blended with **salt, yoghourt, chopped green chilli pepper.**

(2) **Cooked peas,** pressed through a sieve and moistened with **yoghourt** and a suggestion of **hot mango chutney.**

(3) **Leftover curried vegetables,** chopped fine, seasoned with a little **lemon juice** and shredded **coriander leaves.**

(4) **Curd cheese** liquefied with **yoghourt** or **buttermilk,** flavoured with **chilli powder** (or **paprika**), **salt, coriander powder,** fine chopped **spring onions.**

(5) **Pistachios** fried in **ghee,** then lightly salted.

(6) Thick-sliced **tomato** and fine-sliced **sweet onion rings** in a pool of **yoghourt,** decorated with small cut pieces of **mango** (from mango chutney), flavoured with a sprinkling of **coriander powder,** a dusting of **chilli powder,** a few drops of **wine vinegar.**

(7) Peeled **cucumber** in thin slices, seasoned with **salt, lemon juice,** toasted **cummin seed,** and swirled over with **yoghourt.**

(8) Chopped **tomato** and fine grated **apple** mixed with **lime juice,** a little **sugar,** fine minced **onion,** a sprinkle of **garam masala.**

(9) Raw grated **cauliflower,** tossed in **yoghourt, salt,** chopped **green chilli pepper, wine vinegar,** a dash of **chilli powder.**

(10) Grated, sweetened **fresh coconut,** or **desiccated coconut.**

And, as an appropriate end to a stimulating meal, and soothing Indian dessert.

SWEET SEMOLINA HALWA

Prepare **2 tbs. chopped almonds** or **pistachios,** or a combination of both. Fry, together with **1 tbs. seedless raisins,** in a little butter, till raisins swell and nuts are lightly crisped. Transfer to a bowl.

Reheat pan with **2 oz. butter,** then add **4 oz. fine semolina.** Over a gentle heat, stir and fry the semolina till it turns faintly golden. Then add **4 oz. demerara sugar, ¼ tsp. cardamom powder,** and blend through. When thoroughly blended, pour in **1½ cups milk**—slowly—stirring all the while. Continue stirring and cooking gently another 7–10 minutes. Add in a goodly amount of the nuts and raisins, blend well, remove from heat. Fold into glass bowls and allow to cool. Decorate with the remaining nuts and raisins. (Serves 4)

Creatures without feet have my love
And likewise those that have two feet
And those that have four feet I love
And those too that have many feet.
                    attributed to BUDDHA

America

Albert (Alligator), to a rap at the door:
  Who's that knockin' when I is practisin'
  makin' blueberry pies outen carrots an'
  oatmeal?

from *Pogo Possum*
(American comic strip)

America is pre-eminently the land of the snack. And, say some Americans when they are in a self-critical mood, the land of the comic strip. But we needn't take this remark too seriously, even if there is a kind of truth in it. The comic strip is, admittedly, an American phenomenon. A type of social commentary, say some. A hankering after lost innocence—others. The best literature in America today—comic strip readers. The case of Pogo is unique, however. It began as a beautiful idyll in a lush tropical swampland somewhere in an unidentified southern State, where the denizens spend a lot of time reclining up against logs, talking (in folksy dialects), and eating. Definitely a world of innocence where there are only swamp problems to contend with—like the one above, making blueberry pies without blueberries.

Americans, both in and out of comic strips, are an extremely informal people, and a people very conscious about food. Sociable Americans have a habit of "dropping-in" on their friends without notice. So meetings are inevitably accompanied by eating, or snacking. Whether this habit appeals to you or not, there are certainly many times when the thought of preparing a meal is quite wearisome. When you begin to feel this way, it is time to consider the snack.

CHOPPED HERRING WITHOUT HERRING

Hard-boil **2 eggs,** shell and cool. Put through the mincer or chop fine, together with **1½ oz. mild onion, 1 oz. sweet green pepper, 1 oz. peeled tart apple.**

Soak **1 oz. crustless white bread** in **7 tsp. wine vinegar,** mince fine, then mash thoroughly into egg-onion mixture.

Season with **1 rounded tsp. sea-salt, 4 tsp. olive oil,** a dash of **demerara sugar,** a sprinkle of **white pepper.** Blend everything together and pack into a small crock. Leave overnight in the refrigerator. Serve spread on buttered **melba toast** or a variety of **crisp biscuits.**

GOLDY GREEN SPREAD

An excellent one for high teas.

Cook the contents of a small packet of **frozen green beans (4½ oz.)** in a little water till tender. Drain, press out all the liquid.

Fry ¼ **medium Spanish onion,** sliced thin, in **2 tbs. olive oil.** Fry till crisp.

Hard boil a **small egg.** Cool and shell.

Place the green beans, fried onion and egg on a chopping board. Add about 1 tbs. of the oil the onions were fried in, along with some **sea-salt** and a dash of **black pepper.** Now chop till you have a completely creamy purée. Chill till needed. It is tastier left over to the next day.

Both the above preparations are excellent served on *bagels*. These doughnut-shaped bread rolls originated in east Europe, but have long since taken an important place in the national food fair. One of the most agreeable ways of serving them is by first slicing them in half, into two rounds, buttering the cut surfaces very thinly with butter, toasting them under the grill till the butter bubbles and the surfaces turn golden, removing them from the grill and buttering them again (optional), then serving them with morning tea or coffee.

The bagels we have here, usually called *bygels*, are not quite so plump and chewy as their American cousins. They are available daily in many bakeries, at some continental provision stores, in most Jewish bakeries. But try to use them up the same day; otherwise they will qualify for comparison with what was said about a certain very rich, very tight-fisted miser: "His heart is as dry and hard as yesterday's bagels."

MAYFLOWER SALAD

For every 2 portions prepare

　½ **oz. mixed walnuts and almonds**—cut in small pieces
　1 **medium size celery stalk**—chopped small
　1 **oz. stoned dates**—sliced thin
　1 **crisp eating apple**—cored and cut in small chunks
　2 **oz. peeled cucumber**—sliced in thin rounds

dressing

...ain yoghourt
...ld honey
...sh grapefruit juice

...ng smooth.

On each plate arrange some **lettuce** cups. Fill with the mixture of nuts, celery, dates, apple. Spoon over with the dressing and mix through. Distribute round the lettuce cups the slices of peeled cucumber, and on each plate put **3 tbs. creamed sweet corn** and some small mounds of **light cream cheese** like Chambourcy.

AUBERGINE FRITTERS (New Orleans style)

Peel **2 medium size aubergines (12 oz.)** and cut into small chunks. Put to boil in acidulated water till tender—about 15–20 minutes. Drain, squeeze out as much liquid as possible. Mash to a purée. When thoroughly cool, add **2 tsp. sea-salt, 1 egg, 2 tsp. lemon juice, 4 tbs. matzo meal.** Whisk till light and creamy. Drop the mixture by spoonfuls into very hot deep oil and fry till rich golden. Drain on crumpled brown paper. Serve with **lemon wedges** or **Tartare Sauce.** (Serves 4)

TARTARE SAUCE

Add to **4 tbs. good salad cream: 3 tbs. very fine chopped dill-pickled cucumber, 4 tsp. lemon juice, 2 tsp. fine chopped spring onion.** Mix through and let stand for 15 minutes before serving. (4)

BURGERS

Rinse the contents of **1 large tin of gluten** (meatless steaks) in cold water. Squeeze as dry as possible, press firmly between layers of absorbent paper towelling. Put through the mincer into a bowl. Add **2 medium size beaten eggs,** a crushed clove of **garlic, 2 tbs. matzo meal, 1 tsp. sea-salt,** and a little **pepper** if desired. Mix through thoroughly. Wet hands lightly with cold water, form into about 12 fair-sized, fairly thick patties.

Heat some **peanut oil** or **vegetable shmaltz** (p. 150) in a large pan. Fry a medium **Spanish onion** sliced into thin rings. When the onion begins to turn creamy in colour, spread it out to the sides of the pan, add the burgers. Fry on a brisk heat till both sides are crisp and brown. Drain, together with the onion.

Put burgers on split, toasted, round white rolls or baps. Cover with a layer of **fried onion, mustard** and **pickle relish.** Serve with chilled soft drinks or beer, a platter of pickled cucumbers, cole slaw or hot slaw (see below). A perfect late night snack. (Serves 4)

Burgers can also make a more substantial meal. Here are two elaborations:

BURGERS IN THICK BARBECUE SAUCE

Make up a barbecue sauce from the following

- ½ **cup fine minced celery**
- 1 **red chilli pepper**—seeded and chopped fine
- 1 **tbs. chopped sweet pepper** (green or red)
- 2 **tbs. wine vinegar**
- 2 **tbs. soft light-brown sugar**
- 1 **tsp. sea-salt**
- 1 **tbs. soy sauce**
- 2 **tsp. orange juice**
- 1 **tbs. lemon juice**
- ½ **cup tomato ketchup**
- ¼ **cup water**

Amalgamate everything very well.

Have ready: 1 **fine chopped medium onion, 1 large clove of garlic, 1 tsp. fine chopped fresh ginger.**

Heat 1½ **tbs. peanut oil** in a large heavy pan. Add the onion and ginger. Sauté till golden. Reduce heat, follow with the garlic clove, crushed, fry 2 minutes longer. Pour in the barbecue sauce, stir through, cover the pan, simmer 15–20 minutes. Keep hot.

Meanwhile, make up your Burgers (as previously), but minus the onion rings. Turn them out on to heated platters, drench over with the barbecue sauce. Serve together with lots of crisp-fried slender potato chips, bowls of lettuce salad, cold drinks. (Serves 4)

BURGERS IN MUSHROOM SAUCE

Melt **8 tsp. butter,** very slowly and carefully, in a large heavy pan. Add immediately ½ **lb. button mushrooms** cut in halves, 1 **small crushed clove of garlic,** 1 **tsp. sea-salt.** Stir frequently and cook till mushrooms are tender, 5 minutes at most. Remove pan from heat, stir in **5–6 tbs. thick cream, 2 tsp. lemon juice,** ¼ **tsp. dry crumbled dill.** Mix through.

Pour sauce over burgers, serve with portions of cole slaw, and foil-baked potatoes (see below)—split open, buttered and dusted with sea-salt and paprika—and a light red wine. (Serves 4)

SOUR CREAM

Sour cream was introduced into America by emigrants from central Europe. It is now an established culinary ingredient of regional dishes across the land. No doubt this is because of the undeniably creamy and luxurious quality it imparts to whatever is mixed with it. In texture and taste it is something similar to the *crème fraîche* of France, but nowhere as rich and much easier to take. Easier to take, too, than ordinary sweet cream.

It is available here as "sour cream" or "soured cream", and is as versatile in its use as one's own imagination. Add it to salad dressings to mellow them; combine it with sugared fresh strawberries, bananas or other fruit; pour it into avocado halves and mix with fresh herbs; mix with fresh herbs and cold potato slices, or cucumber, or both; swirl it over hot puddings or apple pies; or dip chunks of French bread and vegetables into it. Here's how it helps to "make" our Cole Slaw (Special).

COLE SLAW (SPECIAL)
Anybody can cut up a cabbage,
   dress it and call it "slaw",
But there are kinds so special in taste,
They're special as a guy's own Ma.

   (by an unsung poet of Klondike days,
from a placard in a restaurant window)

Shred fine ¾ **lb. firm white cabbage** and place in a deep bowl. Make up the following dressing:

½ **cup sour cream**
1½ **tbs. wine vinegar**
⅛ **tsp. caraway seed**
1½ **tsp. sea-salt**
1 **tbs. demerara sugar**
1 **rounded tbs. sweet green pepper** cut in short fine strips
¼ **tsp. paprika**

Beat together or shake in a closed bottle till everything is well emulsified. Pour over the cabbage. Stump the cabbage with the butt end of a pestle for a few minutes to help break down the cabbage fibre. Toss and turn well. Cover bowl and let stand in a cool spot for 3–4 hours before serving. Stir occasionally so that the cabbage is always well coated with dressing. (4–6)

HOT HERB SLAW

An interesting variation, but with quite a different character. Shred fine ¾ **lb. firm white cabbage.** Melt **2 tbs. butter** in a large heavy pan, put the cabbage in, stir and fry over a medium heat for 3 minutes, then add a very scant ½ **cup water,** ½ **tsp. dry crumbled dill,** ¼ **tsp. dry crumbled basil,** a pinch **dry crumbled oregano.** Mix through and cover the pan, simmer slowly for 10 minutes. Then add 1½ **tbs. wine vinegar** and **1 tbs. soft light-brown sugar.** Mix through again, simmer another minute and add, finally, **6 tbs. yoghourt.** Stir once again, heat through below simmering point, and serve in a heated glass bowl. (4–6)

PECAN LAYERED CASSEROLE

Of course Americans do have full-sized meals—in between snacking, that is. And here is one of them, very easy to make up, very delightful to eat.

Boil 1½ **lb. potatoes** till *just* tender. Cool, peel, and cut into fairly thin rounds. Then:

cut **2 oz. pecans** into coarse pieces
and ¼ **lb. mushrooms** into fine slices
chop a **small onion (2 oz.)** fine
hard-boil an **egg,** shell and cool
soak an **inch-thick slice of bread,** crust removed, in water. Soak well, then squeeze out and crumble

Heat 1½ **tbs. olive oil** in a small pan. Mellow the mushrooms and onion in it till the onion is turning pale golden. Remove onion and mushrooms from pan and place in a small bowl.

Add the egg, pressed through a sieve, **1 tsp. sea-salt,** a sprinkling of **black pepper,** a pinch of **nutmeg** and one of **dry crumbled basil,** the bread, the pecans. Mix everything together thoroughly, then blend with **1 tbs. vegetable shmaltz.**

Oil liberally the bottom and sides of a medium size casserole with more vegetable shmaltz. Arrange in a layer of potato slices, sprinkle lightly with salt. Cover with a rich layer of mushroom/pecan filling, then another layer of potatoes sprinkled lightly with salt. Continue the process, ending with a layer of potatoes. Drizzle vegetable shmaltz over the top, sprinkle generously with **dry untoasted bread-crumbs.** Bake, uncovered, in a fairly hot oven (375–400°—Gas 5–6) for about 45 minutes, or till top is crisp and golden.

CORN ON THE COB

The term "corn" summons up for Americans what, elsewhere, is known as maize—those beautiful, intricately leaf-encased vegetables with their myriad rows of smiling teeth. The mythology that surrounds corn is so wide-ranging, and ancient, that it is best to omit any special reference to it here. Corn was cultivated by the peoples of the Americas long before the white man came along and thought of putting it up in cans. It was the food of the Inca nobles, and the only one considered worthy of offering to their gods.

It could almost be said that Americans grow up with corn. They get it as "mush" when they're infants, then work up to kernels and to cobs, with corn cakes, corn bread, corn muffins, corn soup, corn syrup, creamed corn and succotash on the way. Many grown-up Americans recall a happy part of their adolescence through the corn roasts they had at summer camp, when the young cobs were spitted through on thin, sharpened green branches and roasted over roaring bonfires, with cheery bouts of communal singing added in. And if they become a little nonchalant or careless of their appearance in later life, they can always turn to corn cob pipes.

Here is a way of preparing corn in one of its most appealing manners. First, buy corn (or maize) only when the teeth are pale golden or milky white—young corn, that is. (This can usually be determined when the shop assistant isn't looking.) The larger and yellower the tooth, the more "corny" the flavour and starchy the texture. Young corn has a subtle sweetness and delicacy all its own.

Allowing **2–3 cobs per person,** remove outer leaves, inner leaves and corn silk. Discard all but a good-sized fistful of the inner leaves. Leave stalks on, if you intend holding the corn in one hand when you eat it later. Let cobs stand in well salted water for 15 minutes or so, then rinse well.

Arrange cobs in the bottom of a large saucepan, cover with a layer of the inner leaves, pour over with a freshly-boiled-up solution of **half milk/half water**—sufficient to cover. Bring back to a light boil, reduce immediately to a faint simmer.

Cook very gently 7–8 minutes. Drain and serve with plenty of **butter,** a sprinkling of **sea-salt** and freshly ground **black pepper.**

Variation: Young corn cobs are also very good grilled. Spread the teeth lightly but thoroughly with butter, put under the grill, turn frequently and baste with more butter, grill till lightly browned.

SWEET CORN FRITTERS

Sieve **2 oz. plain flour** into a bowl together with ½ **tsp. sea-salt.** Make a well in the centre, break in an **egg,** add **4 tbs. milk** and a dash of **pepper.** Mix to a smooth batter, then blend with **2 tbs. tinned sweet corn kernels** (drained). Drop by spoonfuls into **deep hot oil,** cook till both sides are golden, reduce heat and cook a few minutes longer. Drain well. (Serves 2)

NOODLES AND CHEESE

Swedish immigrants to America brought with them their love of dill for practically all flavouring purposes and, like so many other European food habits, it has achieved native-born status.

Bring a large saucepan of water to the boil. Pour in slowly ½ **lb. good quality broad egg noodles** and cook, stirring from time to time, till noodles are just tender. Drain and return to the saucepan and to the heat, the merest suggestion of heat.

Add to the noodles **1 tbs. butter,** and when it melts, ½ **lb. curd or cottage cheese, 2–3 tbs. fresh chopped dill, sea-salt** and **pepper** to taste. Turn and toss gently till everything is well combined. Allow to re-heat a few minutes longer, then serve. (Serves 4)

DILLED NEW POTATOES

Wash or lightly scrub 1½ **lb. small new potatoes.** Steam or boil them in very little water till just tender. Try not to over-cook them—10–12 minutes should be enough. Drain, return to the saucepan and to a gentle heat, give them a heavy sprinkling of chopped **fresh dill,** some **sea-salt** and **pepper, several tbs. butter.** Shake the pan lightly till potatoes are well coated and serve. (4)

CAULIFLOWER À LA KING

A favourite late night snack, but very good luncheon fare too.

Cook a **small cauliflower** in **3½–4 cups water** till tender. Drain, but retain the cooking stock.

Prepare as follows

½ **lb. mushrooms**—cut in medium-size dice
½ **small sweet green pepper**—chopped fine
1–2 small shallots—chopped fine
the cauliflower—cut in small chunks

In a large heavy pan melt **2 tbs. butter** slowly. When it begins to froth, add all the cut-up vegetables, *except the cauliflower*, and fry gently for 5–7 minutes, turning and stirring from time to time. Then add another **tbs. butter** and, just as it melts, sprinkle in **2 tbs. plain flour** and stir till well blended. Now, immediately, pour in a cupful of the cauliflower stock, cook a further few minutes till it thickens, then add the cauliflower. Follow with **2 tsp. sea-salt,** a little **black pepper,** stir again.

Cook slowly a further 3–4 minutes, reduce heat—almost to non-existence—pour in ¼ **cup thick cream.** Mix through, raise heat briefly, serve over thick **toast slices,** sprinkling each portion with **paprika.** For more special occasions, fill **vol-au-vent cases** with the *à la king* mixture. (Serves 4)

FOIL-BAKED POTATOES

Potatoes baked any style are almost universally acceptable. For baking theirs, Americans sometimes fancy those called Idahos, which, like many other things in America, grow really big. An Idaho potato one foot long is no unusual thing to meet with, but a difficulty to struggle through.

Baking in foil has these advantages: it prevents the outer skin from drying out (although the potato itself turns out nicely dry and fluffy); the baking is very even, and the longer it bakes the more "nutty" becomes the flavour. But try to get compost-grown potatoes to enjoy the flavoursome skin as well.

Wash and scrub fairly large **potatoes,** allowing one to a person. Dry, then rub the skins over with **olive oil** and **sea-salt.** Enclose each in a separate piece of aluminium foil, and bake in a hot oven (450°—Gas 8).

Serve with a **large green salad: lettuce leaves** mixed with **batavia leaves** and dressed with **olive oil, wine vinegar** and **sea-salt,** plus individual plates of **cheese chunks** assorted with **black and green olives.** A very healthful and tasty lunch.

HAWAIIAN RICE PINEAPPLE

A sweet-sour rice, pineapple and cabbage mélange—mostly Chinese in background, but American in treatment. An excellent party dish too. The amounts given are for 4–5 servings, but can easily be doubled or trebled as occasion demands. Accompany with plentiful amounts of **tiny burgers** (see above) speared on cocktail sticks, and lots of **cold tropical punch**—equal quantities of **white wine** and a **fruit juice** like **papaya**, for example, then sugared and seasoned with **cloves, lemon peel** twists and some drops of *Elixir Végétal*, with razor-thin rounds of **cucumber** floating on top. Or any other way your inspiration leads you.

blanch 1½ **oz. almonds,** peel, split and fry till light golden (see p. 91—Mushroom Fried Almonds)
shred **6 oz. white cabbage**—shred very fine
chop a **small onion (2 oz.)** rather fine
chop a good slice of **fresh ginger** very fine
make up **1 tbs. chopped sweet green pepper** and **1 tbs. chopped sweet red pepper**

Have ready

2½ **cups dry-cooked rice**—from 1 cup raw (see p. 89)
1 small tin pineapple chunks—drained (4½ oz. net)
¼ **cup of the pineapple syrup**—with ½ **tps. cornflour** dissolved in it
1 large clove of garlic

Heat **2 tbs. peanut oil** in a large pan. Fry onion till golden but not crisp. Remove onion to a warm platter. Crush the garlic clove into the pan, sprinkle in the chopped ginger. Quick-fry and stir for a minute, then follow with the cabbage, the red and green pepper. Fork through, quick-fry and stir over a brisk heat for 4–5 minutes, adding on the way: ½ **tsp. sea-salt, 1½ tsp. soy sauce.** Turn pan contents out on the warmed platter.

Add **1 tbs. more peanut oil** to the pan, heat, put in the rice and pineapple chunks, along with **1 tsp. sea-salt** and **1 tbs. soy sauce.** Fry and stir for a few minutes till heated through, then add the fried vegetables. Mix thoroughly. Add the prepared pineapple liquid and mix through again. Reduce heat and cook a few minutes longer till juice thickens slightly. Blend through with the toasted almond halves, and serve on hot platters. (4–5)

UNION SUIT STEW

During the early decades of this century, when the wintry winds began to blow, and when most Americans relied on other things than central heating to warm their houses, a vogue came in for red flannel underwear, worn mainly by men, and known as the "union-suit"—about which many a ditty and a joke linger on. It was obviously some wit, too, who gave our stew its label, since like its namesake it is bright red and has an admirable action in keeping the cold out.

Heat **2 tbs. olive oil** in a large heavy pan. Fry **1 large chopped onion** in it till lightly brown. Add **2 cups boiled potatoes,** cut in small chunks, **2 cups tinned, drained red beans, 1 small red chilli pepper** (or 2), seeded and finely chopped, **sea-salt** to taste. Cover pan and simmer 15–20 minutes, stir occasionally. (3–4)

SAVOURY NUTS

Nuts prepared this way are an especially good accompaniment to drinks, or just nice for nibbling.

A good mixture would be ½ **cup each** of **pecans, almonds, hazelnuts,** but vary it any way you choose.

Arrange the nuts in a shallow baking tin. Combine **2 tbs. olive oil** with a small bruised **clove of garlic.** Let stand for 20 minutes, remove garlic. Pour oil over nuts, blend and mix well. Sprinkle with **sea-salt.** Bake in a slow to moderate oven until nuts are dry and crisp. Cool.

BANANA MAPLE

When children become blasé about bananas, here is a way of tempting them.

Mash **several ripe bananas** to a creamy consistency, but really creamy, with no lumps in it. Use a silver fork.

Add enough **maple syrup** to sweeten it generously, stir in enough **sour cream** to change the colour to palest beige. Chill, if it's made in summer. Serve in individual glass bowls topped with **crushed walnuts** or **pecans.** Accompany with **thin wafer biscuits.**

ICE-BOX COOKIES

In the days before the refrigerator it was the ice-man who came, walking across the carpets to the kitchen from the street, dripping water from his canvas carrying sack all the while . . .

Ice-box cookies, or, to bring them up to date, refrigerator cookies, are long-standing favourites with Americans of all ages. A type of shortbread, they are very crisp yet melting, rich without being cloying. No matter how generous a supply you make, they are sure to disappear quickly. But they can be made up again at a moment's notice, and they take no more than 7–10 minutes to bake. And the dough will keep in the refrigerator (or ice-box) for up to a week.

Sift together on to a large plate **8 oz. plain flour, 1 tsp. baking powder, ½ tsp. sea-salt.**

In a large bowl cream **3½ oz. butter** till light and creamy. Add **3½ oz. soft light-brown sugar, a scant tsp. vanilla essence,** blend and beat till smooth. Add a medium size **egg,** blend and beat again. Then the flour mixture, stirring and folding till it is all absorbed and a soft dough takes shape. Turn dough out on a well floured board, divide into 3 approximately equal portions. Roll up each, lightly, into cylinders about 6 inches long. Wrap each cylinder separately in foil, place on a flat surface inside the refrigerator. Leave for at least 6 hours before using.

If you wish to elaborate the plain cookie dough, the time to do it is *before* you roll it up into a cylinder and wrap it in foil. For elaborations see below.

Plain Ice-Box Cookies   Remove a roll of cookie dough from the refrigerator, peel away foil carefully. Cut as many cookie rounds as are required—each about ⅛ inch thick. Rewrap unused portion, if any, return to refrigerator without delay. Place cookie slices on an unoiled baking sheet about an inch apart, bake 7–10 minutes in a moderate oven (375°—Gas 5) till light golden brown. Remove cookies from baking sheets with a spatula, cool on a wire rack. Cool completely before storing in a loosely topped jar.

Almond Cookies   Mix **1 portion cookie dough** with **1½ oz. fine chopped almonds.** Blend well, roll up lightly into a cylinder, wrap in foil, store in refrigerator.

Lemon Hazelnut Cookies   Combine **1 portion cookie dough** with **1 oz. chopped hazelnuts** and **½ tsp. grated lemon rind.** Blend, wrap, store in refrigerator.

Cherry Coconut Cookies   Combine **1 portion cookie dough** with **1 tsp. dessicated coconut, 2 tsp. fine chopped maraschino cherries.** Blend, wrap, store.

Love the earth, and sun, and animals.

WALT WHITMAN
(Leaves of Grass)

Greece

They will have olives and cheese and
country stews of roots and vegetables . . .
and they will sip their wine . . . leading
such a healthy and peaceful life they will
naturally live to a good old age.

PLATO (Rep. II)

A recipe for a race of happy Hyperboreans . . . those mythical
people who lived beyond the north north wind in their shel-
tered valleys of plenty? There is, certainly, something of that in
it. But olives, cheese, herbs, and the abundance of vegetables
grown under a Mediterranean sun—together with the pungent
wines of the land—formed the common diet of the Greek
peasant of Plato's time. And the pattern has hardly changed
today. In fact, certain travellers to Greece will even insist to you
that some of Plato's idyll has seeped over into reality when, on
some out-of-the-way country road, they tell of being greeted by
smiling Greek faces and spontaneous gifts of fresh fruit, vegetables and bread.

HONEYED WINE VEGETABLES

The root called *kolokassi*, a patrician cousin of the turnip
which it vaguely resembles—only with an outer covering of
handsome armoured scales and a flavour far more delicate—the
kolokassi is usual for this stew, but new potatoes make an excellent substitute.

Clean the skins of **1 lb. small new potatoes** and cut in
halves. Break off the flowerets of a **small firm cauliflower,**
rinse well in salted water, drain.

Prepare a marinade of the following: **2½ tbs. mild honey,
½ cup dry red wine, 2 tbs. olive oil, 1½ tsp. sea-salt,
1–2 crushed cloves of garlic.** Blend well, then soak the
potato and cauliflower sections in it for an hour. Stir occasionally.

Heat **1½ tbs. olive oil** in a large heavy pan, fry **1 tbs.**

chopped sweet onion till translucent, follow with the potato sections. Mix through and fry over a medium heat, stirring frequently. After 10 minutes add the cut cauliflower and continue frying, and stirring, a further 5 minutes. Now reduce the heat to very low, add 3 tbs. of the marinade, cover the pan, cook gently. After ½ hour add **1 tbs. soy sauce** and **2 chopped spring onions,** re-cover the pan. After 15 minutes more, add 3–4 tbs. of the marinade, leave the pan uncovered now and cook till the vegetables are getting brown and tacky. Remove from heat. (Enough for 4)

Serve with a tangy side-dish like **shredded red cabbage** (dressed in **wine vinegar, olive oil, yoghourt, sugar, salt**) and, if you can get them, the very hard oblong-shaped rolls of **Greek bread,** sesame-dotted and lightly flavoured with aniseed.

Follow with fresh fruit or more yoghourt, or both. Finish with halva, almonds or pistachios, and small cups of Turkish coffee (see p. 144). (Greek halva is one of the best—*Hellas* brand or *Mezap*—being very dry and unoily, subtly sweet and delightfully crumbly. Available in Greek provision stores and many Continental food stores.)

Variation: Almost any other vegetable can be combined with the potato—**young string beans, mushrooms, sugar peas, young carrots, white cabbage.** Use approximately ½ lb. combination vegetable with 1 lb. potato to serve 4.

ASPARAGUS?

Was it Herodotus who first mentioned that the humble radish, when boiled, assumes the more elegant taste of asparagus? Whoever it was, it is an interesting example of "interchangeability of taste". Try it for best results during the summer, when radishes reach their full flavour and are available in big-sized bunches.

Clean **firm medium-large radishes** and place in a saucepan with the barest minimum of water, or better still over a bed of lettuce leaves in a steaming rack. Cook gently for about fifteen minutes, or till tender, then drain and toss in **melted butter** and season with **sea-salt,** a sprinkling of fresh ground **black pepper,** a generous squeeze of **lemon juice.** If the result pleases you, serve as an accompaniment to Sesame Potatoes.

SESAME POTATOES

Boil ¾ **lb. potatoes** in their skins. Peel, mash till completely smooth and velvety. Place in a bowl and add:

6 black olives, stoned and diced, ¼ **tsp. dry crumbled basil, 1 tsp. sea-salt, 1 scant tbs. butter, 2 tbs. matzo meal.** Mix well together, then form into medium size patties. Press each side lightly into a mound of **sesame seeds.** Fry the patties on a hot, lightly-oiled griddle till pale brown on both sides. Add a little more oil from time to time. Then pile them into a warmed pottery bowl and surround with a combination of **red and green sweet peppers** and **onion,** sliced in fine rings and mellowed in **olive oil; Asparagus?** (as above) or coarsely grated unpeeled **radish,** salted and mixed with **yoghourt;** young **spring onions** split lengthwise; and, for variety at other times, **Smoked Aubergine.** (3)

> We pickle them as babies . . . and roast them when they're getting big and fat . . . and, when they're old, we fry them! What would we do without our friend the aubergine?
>
> (Greek country saying)

SMOKED AUBERGINE

The "babies" we may buy from time to time in Greek food stores. They are usually stuffed with strips of red pepper (hot), celery and carrot, and flavoured by an agreeably-spiky pickle solution. It is the "big and fat" ones that concern us here.

Prepare one of these **plump aubergines (weight 8–10 oz.)** as you would for Mouzhik's Caviar (p. 62), up to the point where you have placed it on the chopping board and have removed as many seeds as possible.

Now add **1½–2 tbs. raw sliced Spanish onion, 1 good tsp. fresh parsley,** and begin chopping. From time to time add small amounts of **olive oil, red wine vinegar** and **sea-salt** and, as they are absorbed, keep chopping. The final result should be a smooth purée, saturated but not flowing in liquid, and with a smoky, rather tangy, flavour.

If put up in sterilized jars, Smoked Aubergine will last the winter. But make sure to float enough oil over the surface, enough even to let it spill out slightly when you cap the jar down.

AUBERGINE BABY OMELETTES

Peel and mince fine into a bowl: **1 medium size aubergine (8 oz.), 1 small onion (2 oz.).** Add 1½ **tbs. sea-salt,** let stand for 20–25 minutes, drain and squeeze out most of the liquid possible, return to the bowl. Now add: **3 beaten eggs, 1 tbs. plain flour.** Beat till light and frothy.

Heat ¼ **inch depth of olive oil** (or **peanut oil**) in a large heavy pan. Drop aubergine/egg mixture into the hot oil in large soup-spoonfuls, fry till really brown on both sides. Drain well on absorbent paper, serve immediately with **lemon wedges** and with a large salad bowl containing: **quartered tomatoes,** crisp **lettuce hearts, radishes, celery curls, black and green olives,** dressed with a **light mayonnaise** whipped through with fresh **coriander leaves** and **lemon juice.** (Serves 4)

OLIVES

The olives one usually sees on delicatessen counters everywhere are fairly large, briny tasting, and vary in colour from dark brown to black. If the quality is good one can be reasonably certain they are Greek (although this is not to cast a slur on other olive growing countries like France and Morocco, which produce excellent though smaller varieties). These bigger olives will probably have originated in the districts of Amfissa or Volos on the mainland of Greece. They are the "money-makers" of the olive world, and are graded in size from medium to huge. They are also the type most useful when it comes to making up olive spreads, pastes, etc. There are also many other types, since olive production in Greece—going back to the days of antiquity—is a highly sophisticated culture. For example, there are the *calamatas*, which come, as one would expect, from the Calamata district on the Peloponnese. These exquisite-tasting and more highly priced creatures are a beautiful dark purple in colour, pointed at either end and, to suit their higher station in life, preserved in olive oil and wine vinegar. You may sometimes find them in Greek shops on trays; more often they are available only in tins. Another type sometimes met with in Greek shops, although more rarely since their production is limited, are the *roupades*—small, often wizened, creamy textured and smoky tasting olives—considered by many Greeks to be the queen of the lot. *Roupades* grow on Chios, Lesbos and Cyprus. Unlike other varieties, which cannot be eaten unless they are first marinated, *roupades*, before they are fully ripe, are affected by a beneficial fungus (no doubt laid on them by some kindly god in ancient days), and fall from the trees all ready to eat. They are preserved in olive oil.

Generally speaking, olives are only expensive when they are bought in bottles or tins. When they are bought loose, particularly in Greek shops, they are amazingly cheap. A certain Russian acquaintance, a man of heroic proportions and excessively advanced age, claims to this day that his indestructibility is due to his having consumed each morning for breakfast a half-pound of black olives along with a pint of dark beer and a chunk of black bread. All of which was put away in a local vegetarian restaurant in Odessa where the motto was "We don't eat anyone here!". (So much for formulas on longevity.)

OLIVES AND CHEESE

A simply prepared but admirable late evening meal when combined with a salad of sliced radish and cucumber, lightly oiled and salted, and glasses of chilled white wine.

Cut ½ **lb. bland, firm cheese** into ½-inch cubes. Cut **12–15 black olives** into halves—remove pits. Fry both in **1 tbs. butter** till the cheese cubes become creamy and frothy on several sides. Turn cheese cubes frequently, and the olives once. Now add **1 tbs. white wine** and let everything cook gently a further 2 minutes. Stir through, remove from heat, spoon quickly on to thick slices of **buttered white bread.** Sprinkle with **paprika** or fresh ground **black pepper.** (Serves 3)

OLIVES AND EGGS

Stone **2 oz. black olives** and put through a fine mincer. Hard-boil an **egg,** shell and cool. Discard about a quarter of the egg white, put the remaining white and yolk through the mincer as well. Combine the minced ingredients on a chopping board and reduce to a smooth purée by chopping, adding in the process **2 tbs. olive oil,** 1½ **tsp. lemon juice,** some pinches of **sea-salt** (if the olives are not too briny-tasting already), and a sprinkling of **chopped fresh or crumbled dry basil.** Refrigerate till needed and serve thickly spread on **hot toasted**

bread fingers. Decorate with **cut olive halves. 1 tbs. or so of fried onion** can also be added to the ingredients before chopping.

Olives and Eggs is only one of a numerous variety of *mèze*, the hors d'oeuvres served in the *tavernas* of Greece, where a large tray of them is inevitably passed round with the drinks. Other typical *mèze* are green and black olives, our miniature friends the "baby" aubergines, pickled mushrooms, *fava*, flavoury rice stuffed into vine leaves, salted chick peas (see *Nahit*), *taramasalata*, salted curd cheese, *tahine* (a thick and creamy sauce widely used throughout the Mediterranean, made from sesame seeds and flavoured with garlic and herbs and used as a bread dip), and many many more.

"TARAMASALATA"

Our Taramasalata comes equipped with a pair of inverted commas to distinguish it from the other kind, made from smoked fish roes.

And since we are now beginning to exhaust such terms as "intriguing" and "smoky-tasting", let us content ourselves with the merely "delicious".

Stone **4 oz. large black olives** and put through a mincer into a mortar. Add **2½ tsp. lemon juice, 1½ tsp. sea-salt, 2 tbs. soft fresh bread-crumbs.** Pound and mix till the whole mass is well amalgamated, then serve on slices of **hot buttered toast.** Sprinkle over with fine minced **sweet onion.** (Enough for 7–8 toast slices)

FAVA

Aristophanes tells us that the mighty Herakles, who was not very fussy about what he ate, was, however, particularly fond of a sort of purée made of mashed beans. And if the strain of such spectacular heroes has diminished over the ages, the dish at least has improved in flavour.

Soak ½ **lb. dried broad beans** for 24 hours in plenty of water mixed through with **1 tsp. bicarbonate of soda.** Drain, put to simmer in a saucepan of water, along with a chopped medium size **onion.** When beans are completely tender, drain them and the onion, cool, then pass through a fine sieve (discard residue). Add: **5 tbs. olive oil, 1½–2 tsp. sea-salt,** the juice of a **large lemon,** 2–3 tsp. **fine chopped parsley,** a sprinkling of **white pepper.** Whip the mixture till light and frothy. Chill. Serve piled into a colourful pottery bowl, swirl up the surface. Excellent as an appetizer, or as a dip for hot toast chunks. (Enough for 8)

PICKLED MUSHROOMS

Clean ½ **lb. small button mushrooms,** white and absolutely fresh. Leave whole if *very* small, otherwise cut in halves. Trim stems.

Simmer a mixture of the following in a small saucepan for 5 minutes: ½ **cup wine vinegar, ¼ cup water, 4 tsp. olive oil, 1 tsp. sea-salt, ½ tsp. mixed coriander and dill seed, 2 tsp. mild honey, ½ bay-leaf,** crumbled.

Drop the mushrooms in and simmer 5–6 minutes more. Then skim out mushrooms and remove to a bowl, and continue cooking the liquid, briskly, a further 5 minutes. Pour over mushrooms and allow to cool. (4–6)

ARTICHOKES

The enjoyment of eating artichokes depends not only on choosing this nobly-shaped vegetable when its leaves are firm and green and moist, but also on the delicate flavour of the dressing into which the base of each leaf is dipped. Artichokes are best eaten entirely cold.

Allowing **1 medium size artichoke** per person, rinse the artichokes thoroughly in salted water, spreading the leaves gently apart so that any sand or grit floats away. Then put to boil in a large saucepan of water and cook to the point at which a leaf, when pulled, comes away easily (about 20–25 minutes). Drain and allow to cool.

Basic dressing Pulverize ¾ **tsp. sea-salt** and ½ **tsp. dry oregano** to a smooth powder in a mortar. Add ½ **small clove of garlic,** pound to liquid and amalgamate. Stir in ½ **tsp. mild honey** and amalgamate again. Then ½ **tsp. lemon juice,** and work in any of the mixture which clings to the sides of the mortar. Now **5 tbs. olive oil,** bit by bit, stirring quickly and absorbing it before adding more. Then **2–3 tsp. wine vinegar** and some quick final spins in the mortar. (Enough to dip 3–4 artichokes)

Variations: (1) If the basic dressing is a bit too rich for you, thin it down with **cream** or **yoghourt.**
(2) Substitute oregano with **basil,** or garlic with **1 tsp. fine minced onion.**

(3) Use **Green Aioli** (p. 57) thinned down with **yoghourt.**

Taking a leaf off at a time, dipping the fleshy base into the dressing, then easing this delicacy off between your teeth, you will eventually come to the stubbly centre or "choke" of the vegetable which, when you scrape it away, will reveal the "heart"—reputedly its choicest part. Cut the "heart" away from the stalk, trim it, dip it in the dressing and eat it.

Artichokes are virtually a summer meal in themselves, if accompanied with bread and butter, chunks of creamy cheese, and light red wine.

BABY MARROWS YAHNI STYLE

Wash **1 lb. baby marrows** (courgettes), cut off the ends but don't peel, slice into ½-inch rounds, sprinkle with **sea-salt,** put in a sieve under a weight for about an hour. Rinse and pat dry.

Heat **3 tbs. olive oil** in a heavy pan, add **3 coarsely chopped spring onions.** Fry for a minute or two, then follow with **4 smallish tomatoes (6 oz.),** skinned and chopped, **1 large crushed clove of garlic,** ½ tsp. **coriander seed,** lightly bruised, **1 small bay-leaf,** ⅛ tsp. **paprika,** ¼ **cup cold water.** Let it all simmer slowly for 5–6 minutes, then add the marrows and **1 tsp. sea-salt.** Shake the pan, cover, cook gently for 25 minutes or till tender. When done, squeeze in **1 tps. lemon juice.**

Serve hot over beds of **dry-cooked rice** (p. 89) or cold with lots of **green salad.** (3–4)

LEMON SOUP

And if you have any rice left over try this.

Beat the yolk of **1 very fresh egg** in a small bowl together with **1 tbs. lemon juice.**

Flavour **1½ pints briskly boiling water** with **3¾ tsp. Instant Soup powder** (or to taste). Add **3–4 tbs. cooked rice** to the soup, stir, remove from heat. Spoon the soup, little by little, into the egg yolk/lemon juice mixture, stirring constantly. Continue the process till about half the soup is used up, then transfer the bowl contents back to the saucepan, stirring again and blending thoroughly. Re-warm on an extremely gentle heat, season with a little fresh ground **black pepper.** Be careful not to let the soup boil again, or the egg may curdle. Serve hot, sprinkled over with **chopped fresh parsley;** or chilled, with **thin cucumber slices** floating on top. (3–4)

DOUBLE-DRESSED POTATO SALAD

Boil **2 lb. waxy potatoes** till tender, peel, keep warm.

Make up dressings (1) Pulverize in a mortar **1 tsp. sea-salt, ¼ tsp. dry thyme** to a smooth powder. Add **2 small strips lemon rind** (zest), **½ crushed clove garlic.** Pound and amalgamate well. Now add **1 tsp. mild honey** and blend, then **½ tsp. lemon juice** and **2 tsp. wine vinegar,** stirring in well. Finally, **2 tbs. olive oil,** stirring and mixing everything together.

(2) Heat a little **olive oil** in a small frying pan. Fry **4 tbs. diced sweet onion** and **4 tbs. diced sweet green pepper,** till onions are lightly brown.

Slice potatoes into ¼-inch-thick slices, arrange in a heated bowl. Pour over with Dressing (1), mix through. Stir through with Dressing (2). Serve hot. (Enough for 4–5)

FAKÈS

Fakès (or **lentils,** simply), which are sold at Greek provision stores, are usually shining golden in colour, very thin, fast cooking, and delicate in flavour.

Wash **½ lb. split golden lentils,** the thinner the better, in several changes of cold water. Put in a saucepan with **2 cups water,** bring to the boil, skim the surface if necessary, simmer very slowly for 20 minutes. Add **1½ tsp. sea-salt, ⅛ tsp. mustard seed, ½ tsp. coriander powder, 1 crushed garlic clove.** Stir and continue simmering till the lentils are tender. Crush lentils in the pot lightly with a potato masher, remove from heat, keep very warm.

Fry **½ small chopped sweet onion** in a little **olive oil** till light brown. Add onion and oil to the lentils, mix through, serve in individual bowls. Accompany with a large **lettuce salad,** combined with generous amounts of chopped fresh **coriander leaves,** and dressed with **lemon juice, olive oil** and **sea-salt;** a plate of **Smoked Aubergine;** a bowl of **calamata olives.** (4)

SKORDALIA

This thick lemony sauce goes beautifully with boiled or steamed vegetables like new potatoes, young cauliflower or beetroot, baby carrots, tender green beans. It can also be used as a filling for avocado halves, or for the hollows of crisp young celery stalks.

Macerate **1 small clove of garlic** in a mortar together with **1 tsp. sea-salt.** Add **1 oz. fresh ground almonds, 1 tbs. lemon juice.** Pound and blend to a creamy paste. Now add **4 tbs. olive oil,** slowly, so that it is constantly being absorbed. Stir briskly till the mixture is smooth and palest beige in colour. (Enough for 4)

Skordalia can be prepared far in advance and refrigerated till needed.

*   *   *

There is a tale that the poet Arion was saved from the sea by the intervention of a dolphin, which carried him on its back to the shore. There are many other antique tales like this, and for years scholars discounted them as being absurd or purely fanciful. But nowadays the range and complexity of dolphin language (once described by Aristotle) is a source of continuing astonishment to us. And whatever these highly cerebral creatures get up to, we no longer doubt their capacity or intelligence.

We read that Thales was once called upon to match wits with a mule—a highly ingenious animal, a carrier of bags of salt (but not by inclination). It had learned, when fording daily through a stream, that it could lighten its burden by bending its knees, so that the water, coming into contact with the salt, would wash most of it away. In the end Thales won. We should be very disappointed if he hadn't—after all, he was considered one of the seven wise men of Greece.

Throughout their writings the ancients show a very lively interest in animal behaviour. In our own day some of that same interest is rapidly reviving.

Near East

Fruits and nuts play a large part in the lands and literatures of the Near East. The symbol of fruit, representing the beauty—and the snares—of womankind, became with time an overworked one. Nonetheless, some of man's most ingenious and poetic metaphors have evolved this way. It is a sorry day in the Near East which does not include some portion of fruits and nuts. Fruits and nuts like the fresh purple fig, the sweet juicy melon, the golden apricot, the almond, the green-hued pistachio—all of which can be combined into a salad fit for a Caliph.

ANATOLIA FRUIT SALAD

For **1 medium size sweet melon** have **3 ripe apricots, 2 purple (fresh) figs, 1 oz. almonds, $\frac{1}{2}$ oz. pistachios.** Lightly toast and crush the nuts and set aside.

Cut the melon flesh and purple figs into small chunks, peel and slice the apricots. Put the fruit into a bowl, make up a dressing:

Blend **3–4 tsp. mild honey** with **1 tbs. lemon juice,** the juice of **1 medium size tart-sweet apple, 2 tbs. heavy cream,** a few drops of *Elixir Végétal.* Blend well, pour over and mix through the fruit lightly. Chill.

Serve up in glass bowls, topped with the crushed nuts, and with an accompaniment of **thin wafer biscuits.** (Serves 4–5)

DATE-SUGARED APPLES

Take firm, sweet, red **apples**—one per serving. Core and dip immediately into a bowl containing water, a generous squeeze of **lemon juice,** a flavouring of **rose or orange flower essence.** Cut each apple petal-wise round the rim, return to the lemon water solution. Make up this mixture:

Put in a mortar **2 oz. stoned dates.** Pound and mash well. Then **1 tsp. chopped seedless raisins,** and amalgamate. Then **6 tbs. plain yoghourt, 1 tbs. soft light-brown sugar, $\frac{1}{8}$ tsp. cinnamon, $\frac{1}{8}$ tsp. cardamom powder.** Stir and blend thoroughly. (Enough for 4–5 medium size apples)

Drain apples, set on a plate, fill and stuff with the mixture. Cover and chill. Serve with a topping of **crushed toasted almonds.**

"He is now seated between two houris drinking milk and honey . . ."* Thus do they try to console Hajji Baba when he returns to Ispahan only to learn that his father, the barber, is no more. In the East, milk and honey have come to symbolize the ultimate in peace and plenty, and form the basis of many oriental sweetmeats.

HASHMERIM

A Turkish sweet.

Combine about **4 tbs. mild-flavoured honey** with **1–1½ tsp. orange flower essence.** Toast **1 oz. pistachios** under the grill, allow to cool, then crush coarsely. Prepare **1½ tsp. fresh grated lemon rind.**

Crumble **1 lb. cottage cheese** into a large heavy pan and set on a very low heat. Stir till half-melted. Add ½ **oz. plain flour,** and continue stirring till a suggestion of liquid begins to run from the cheese. Remove from heat immediately, add the honey mixture and the grated lemon rind. Blend through. Spoon into warmed bowls and top each portion with the crushed toasted pistachios. (4–6)

YOGHOURT

Making one's own yoghourt at home is not only more economical, but the result obtained has a freshness and tang that is often lacking in the ordinary commercial product. More digestible than either milk or cream, yoghourt shows its worth in the variety of its uses.

When whipped cream is called for, yoghourt sweetened with soft brown sugar is far less cloying and fattening.

Stirred in with sliced cucumbers, fresh chopped herbs, a flavouring of sea-salt and garlic, it creates a *Balkan Cucumber Salad.*

Added to chunkily cut apples, with a sprinkling of chopped nuts and brown sugar, it makes for a quick and satisfying breakfast (see p. 165).

Mixed with a platter of torn lettuce leaves, sliced radish, chopped spring onion, cottage cheese and sea-salt, it contributes to an absolutely delicious and refreshing *Summer Salad.*

* from *Hajjia Baba of Ispahan* by James Morier (1780–1849).

Put into a double thickness of butter muslin and allowed to drain overnight, it becomes yoghourt cheese, a velvety creamy cheese perfect for spreading on thin slices of rye bread or crackers. To store: shape into small balls, put in an appropriate sized glass bottle, fill to the top with olive oil, cap. The cheese will keep this way indefinitely, refrigerated or not.

On its own, simply sweeten yoghourt with treacle, barbados sugar, honey, fruit conserve or maple syrup, and serve at breakfast or as a dessert.

To make yoghourt: put **2 pints best quality milk** into a clean saucepan. Bring to the boil and let bubble just once. Remove from heat and transfer to a glass bowl, a heavy glass casserole preferably. Allow to cool to blood heat (98–100°), or just sufficiently for the inside of your wrist to take a few drops comfortably. Add in, immediately, **3 tsp. fresh store-bought yoghourt**—the better the quality, the better your result. Stir with a glass rod or clean spoon. Now cover the bowl with a plate, or the casserole with its lid. Enclose the whole in layers of thick towel or blanket, or anything that will provide enough insulation to keep the milk from cooling too quickly. Store in a warm place. Or, if you're more enterprising, put the yoghourt-indoctrinated milk into smaller glass bowls, and then in an insulated wooden box. Cover each bowl with a layer of butter muslin. Set a kettle or pot of freshly boiled water in the centre. Put a lid over the box, insulate with a rug or heavy blanket. (This latter method will ensure a steady irradiation of warmth for most of the "culturing" period.) Either way, your yoghourt will "set" in about 8–10 hours, and you will have a largish quantity on hand to see you through 4–5 days, providing it is kept cool or refrigerated. Reserve 3 tsp. as a starter for your next batch. Eventually, after about five or six times, you will have to re-start your yoghourt with a new supply from the store.

IM-HASHA

(Which in Arabic simply means "stuffed", and is less involved than it looks.)

Use carrots just big enough to be cored, medium size tomatoes, small round turnips and beetroots (raw), courgettes—say, two of everything, plus a large sweet Spanish onion and 12 white grapes.

Carrots—scrape and core, leaving outer thickness of about ¼ inch.

Tomatoes—cut off caps, hollow out centres.

Turnips and **beetroots**—scrape, cut off caps, hollow out centres, leaving outer thickness of about ¼ inch.

Courgettes—core from end to end.

Onion—pop into freshly boiling water for 7 minutes, take out, cool. Make an incision, on one side, from the stem down to the root, peel away the larger layers intact, about five such layers will do. Put the layers into the boiling water and cook gently for 3 minutes, or till just pliable, skim out and drain.

Grapes—cut in half lengthwise and remove seeds.

Mince or chop fine the scooped out portions of all the vegetables, together with about **half the heart of the onion.** Add a good-sized handful of raw **patna rice** (something less than ½ cup), **2 large cloves of crushed garlic, 2 tsp. sea-salt, 1 scant tsp. coriander powder.** Blend well together.

Stuff the chopped mixture lightly into the hollowed out vegetables, replacing the caps on the tomatoes, beetroots, turnips. In the case of the courgettes and carrots, allow the mixture to fall short of the ends by about ½ inch. Fill each layer of onion with 1 tbs. of the remaining mixture. Fold over envelopewise. Carefully arrange all the vegetables in a large well-oiled pan, add ½ **tsp. crushed coriander seed,** drizzle everything over with **olive oil.** Cover pan and set on a low heat.

After about 20 minutes of cooking time, add the juice of **1 small lemon** in which **2 tsp. demerara sugar** have been well dissolved. After about 35 minutes of cooking time, turn the vegetables carefully over, and again in a further 35 minutes approximately. Now add the grapes, skin sides up, in the spaces between the vegetables. Turn everything a few times more. Total approximate cooking time: 1¾ hours.

The final result should have the appearance of a bazaar of variegated glazed fruits, with the colour of the beetroot infusing everything with streaks of red. Serve cold, arranged on a platter, with glasses of chilled white wine. (You will find that, because of the rice, all the vegetables, including the tomatoes, slice firmly and beautifully.) Serves 4.

SKEWERED VEGETABLES

Porphyrius once said that even if all the wolves and vultures in the world approved the use of meat, we could not be convinced it was right. Throughout the Near East (and Balkans) vegetables like aubergines, marrows, onions, sweet peppers, mushrooms, tomatoes, by their very abundance often provide delicious substitutes for meat. A particularly tasty way of serving these vegetables, and keeping their flavours distinct, is by grilling them or charcoal-broiling them on skewers till lightly crisp and savoury.

Peel and cut **1 medium size aubergine (8 oz.)** into 1-inch cubes. Core and seed **1 medium size sweet green or red pepper,** cut into 1-inch squares. Parboil both vegetables in well salted water for 3–4 minutes only, drain and cool.

Prepare the rest of the vegetables

6 small, firm, slightly green tomatoes—cut into halves
8 very small shallots—remove outer skins, leave whole
¼ lb. firm button mushrooms—clean, remove stalks

Make up a marinade: **3 tbs. olive oil, 6 tbs. medium-sweet sherry, 6 tbs. soy sauce, 1 tbs. honey, 1 tsp. sea-salt, 1 large crushed garlic clove.** Amalgamate well. Marinate all the vegetables for about 1 hour, then arrange on individual skewers, alternating aubergine, pepper, tomato, pepper, shallot, mushroom—till the skewers are full. Dredge lightly with **flour,** set under a grill or over a charcoal fire, turn fairly frequently, baste occasionally with the remaining marinade, grill till tender and slightly charred.

Serve the skewers over beds of **dry-cooked rice,** accompany with **lemon wedges.** (4–6)

NAHIT

Soak **¾ lb. dried chick peas** overnight in cold water, to which has been added **½ tsp. bicarbonate of soda.** Drain and rinse and put to boil till tender (approximately 2 hours). Drain again, very well, turn out on a large clean tea-towel, spreading them so that there is only one layer. Sprinkle immediately with **sea-salt** and freshly ground **black pepper** and leave till cold. These Nahit make an appetizing tidbit or an excellent accompaniment to drinks. (6–8)

SPICED GLUTEN KEBAB

If you are feeling really "orientally-minded", take a **large can of gluten** (meatless steaks) and do as follows.

Rinse the pieces of gluten in cold water and squeeze as dry as possible. The optimum thickness for our purpose is about ¼ inch, so you may have to slice some of the thicker pieces accordingly.

Cover the surface of each piece with a generous sprinkling of **mixed pickling spice,** together with a dash of sea-salt and some slivers of **raw garlic.**

Cut squares of aluminium foil, a little larger than gluten size, and according to number. Now roll up each gluten piece so that the contents are well enclosed, wrap firmly round with a square of foil, twist the ends tight. Place in the freezer compartment of your refrigerator for 48 hours.

Remove from refrigerator and allow to thaw a little—a few minutes only. Strip off the foil, but do not try to unroll. Dip each of the pieces into **beaten egg** flavoured with **soy sauce.** Fry over a brisk heat in a thinly oiled pan, till the egged surfaces are nicely golden. The thawing process should now be almost complete. Spread open carefully and fry till lightly crisp on the spiced side. Drain on brown paper. Remove pieces of spice and garlic and serve—with **pickled vegetables** (usually available at Greek provision stores), or **green salad** or **Sesame Potatoes** (p. 129). (4)

MILLET

Millet is a grain which receives more appreciable notice than any other in the writings of the ancient world. Why is this? Probably because it is one of the easiest crops to cultivate, and because the number of "ears" per stalk is so plenteous. Millet-eating has declined to a great extent in our own day, although many birds continue to enjoy its flavour. There was a theory current at one time that the reason why men in the north of China were so tall, and those in the south, well, not so tall, was that they cultivated millet in the north and rice in the south. With the advent of new interest in the matter of what we eat and why, a new "cultus" of millet-eating is beginning to emerge. Russian athletes are said to train on an almost exclusive diet of millet porridge (recipe unknown), and everyone knows what Russian athletes are like. All this makes millet sound like one of those nasty-tasting things which are only "good" for one. In fact, millet is an extremely simple food to prepare and has a unique nut-like flavour of its own. Excellent varieties of millet are obtainable at most health food counters throughout the country. Some Polish delicatessen shops stock it under the name of "yellow kasha".

MILLET PILAFF

Wash **1 cup millet** in several changes of water till the water

runs clear, then drain. Heat **1 tbs. olive oil** in a large pan, add
the millet, fry till golden over a medium heat, turning the grains
occasionally. Pour in **¾ cup cold water,** allow to steam up,
follow with **1 tsp. sea-salt, 1–1½ tbs. soy sauce,** a **small
crushed clove of garlic.** Cook gently till all the water is
absorbed, when the grains should appear separate and dry.
Flavour further with chopped fresh herbs like **borage** or **basil,**
some finely chopped **spring onions,** thin slices of raw **button
mushrooms,** young sweet uncooked **green peas.** Stir and
heat through well, serve at once. (4)
This dish goes very nicely with a platter of Lemon Cucumbers.

LEMON CUCUMBERS

The **cucumbers** must be perfectly fresh and firm. Peel, slice
thin, arrange in one layer over a plate. Sprinkle lightly with
sea-salt, a generous squeeze of **lemon juice,** a discreet amount
of chopped **fresh mint.** Leave to stand for 15 minutes before
serving.

THE IMAM'S MOUSTACHE

There was an Imam, so the story goes, whose passion was a
certain kind of millet pilaff blazoned with numerous herbs,
fruits and other delicacies. Even during his devotions he would
dip into a pouch he kept slung at his waist and fill his mouth
copiously and secretively. While no one had ever actually seen
him in the act—he had a way, apparently, of making some
pious movement toward his mouth during which a lump of
pilaff was skilfully inserted—the tell-tale evidence remained . . .
in his beard, around his whiskers, even, some malicious
tongues said, around the corners of his eyes. Fortunately, it
happened to be in Persia, where senses of humour and taste are
well developed. Accordingly, the Imam's guilty secret was
exposed but, as punishment, he was only compelled to reveal
the ingredients. The name of the dish became, appropriately,
The Imam's Moustache, and as nearly as can be reconstructed
it went something like this:
Prepare **1 cup of millet** as for Millet Pilaff—inclusive of
sea-salt, soy sauce, garlic—up to the point where all the
water has been absorbed. Transfer to a deep bowl and let cool.
Meanwhile, fry **¼ cup sliced sweet onion rings** in **1½
tbs. olive oil** till onions are crisp and golden. Drain. Toast **1 oz.
almonds** and **½ oz. pistachios** lightly under the grill. Watch

that they do not burn. When cool, crush into small pieces. Chop
1 tbs. seedless raisins very fine.

Add onion rings, nuts and raisins to millet and blend
through. Portion off into individual bowls, decorate with a few
chopped **coriander (or mint) leaves.** (Serves 4)

Accompany with small relish side-dishes like **thick-sliced
tomato** lightly tossed in **wine vinegar; grated radish**
dressed in **olive oil** and **sea-salt;** coarsely **grated cauliflower**
in **yoghourt** flavoured with **chilli powder.** Follow with cups
of velvety Turkish Coffee.

TURKISH COFFEE

The "Turkish" in Turkish Coffee is merely a convenient term
for a way of preparation. According to one version, it was the
Turks in fact who introduced coffee-drinking to Europe—not
that they had planned it that way. When the Turks were
finally driven off from Vienna in 1683 (mainly due to the
intervention of King John Sobieski of Poland), they left behind
in their abandoned baggage the implements and ingredients for
coffee-making. The ingenious Viennese soon discovered their
use, with the result that very soon after the habit became
wildly popular and the first coffee-houses in Europe were set
up.

It is preferable, as with any other style of coffee-making, to
use freshly roasted beans which can be pulverized in a coffee
grinder immediately beforehand. Otherwise, ask your coffee
merchant to grind a small amount of your favourite after-
dinner variety "Turkish" style, that is, to powder.

Use a "Turkish" coffee pot—obtainable in various sizes in
Greek provision stores, or in the kitchenware section of depart-
ment stores.

Add **freshly boiled water** to your "Turkish" coffee pot,
according to the number of cups (small coffee cups) required,
plus a generous tsp. or more of **demerara sugar** per cup.
Don't stint the sugar—Turkish coffee should be sweeter than
usual. Bring back to the boil, remove from heat, add in the
powdered coffee—2 tsp. per cup. Shake the pot gently to
and fro so that all the coffee is absorbed and a creamy froth
forms. Return to the heat, allow to come to the boil again,
remove. Let stand 1–2 minutes. Just before serving give the pot
a few more gentle shakes. Serve black, or, if you prefer, with a
small addition of rich cream.

APRICOT "BOURGHOUL"

Shredded wheat can taste remarkably like a kind of wheat much eaten in the Near East—*bourghoul*. The recipe below is for a bourghoul in the pilaff style, and makes a particularly light and enjoyable meal.

Wash **1 tbs. seedless raisins** and cut into halves. Soak **4 small dried apricots** in **hot water** for 10 minutes. Drain and slice in thin strips.

Heat **2 tbs. olive oil** in a heavy frying pan and let it get quite hot. Add **1 small onion (2 oz.)** in thin slices, fry till just beginning to turn golden. Follow with **2 crushed cloves of garlic** and stir.

Meanwhile, put **4 shredded wheat biscuits** into a bowl and cover with **cold water**—for 15–20 seconds *only*. Drain immediately, squeeze out well. Tear into smallish pieces.

Now add the shredded wheat to the onion and garlic and blend through. Continue frying on a rather high heat about 5 minutes, turning pieces frequently. Add raisins and apricots and mix everything together. Sprinkle over with **1 tbs. soy sauce.** Press surface down lightly with the back of a spatula. Reduce heat a little and let cook till underside has become crisp and light brown, adding a little more oil if necessary. Turn wheat over, allow the other side to crisp up, serve. (2)

Arrange on hot platters and top with **toasted crushed almonds.** Serve with relish side-dishes of **sweet onion and sweet red pepper rings** mellowed in **olive oil** and flavoured with **coriander powder,** thin sliced **cucumber** dressed in **yoghourt** and seasoned with **sea-salt.**

ALMONDS AND MARROWS

Wash but don't peel **1 medium size vegetable marrow (1½–2 lb.).** Cut into half crosswise and boil gently for 12–15 minutes. Drain, cool, then cut each half lengthwise, giving you 4 marrow quarters. Scoop out the centre of each quarter and reserve 3 of these scooped out portions. Remove any large seeds.

Prepare a filling:

pulverize **1 oz. almonds** in your electric coffee grinder
soak an **inch-thick slice of bread,** crust removed, in water for a few minutes, then squeeze out well

peel a large ripe **tomato,** slice thin, sprinkle lightly with sugar
chop or mince fine the **3 portions of marrow centre**

Heat **1 tbs. olive oil** in a heavy pan. Add **1 tbs. chopped sweet onion.** Fry for a minute, then follow with **a crushed clove of garlic, ½ tsp. lightly crushed coriander seed.** Stir for a few moments before adding the ground almonds, the soaked bread, well crumbled, the chopped marrow centres, and **½ tsp. sea-salt, ½ tsp. coriander powder.** Mix together very well as you continue to fry another 3 minutes. Remove from heat and allow to cool. Add **a small beaten egg** to the mixture and amalgamate.

Sprinkle the surfaces of the marrow quarters with **sea-salt,** then lay a few slices of tomato in each hollow. Top up the centres generously, but lightly, with the fried mixture. Arrange the stuffed marrows on a well oiled baking sheet. Drizzle the tops over with olive oil, bake for approximately 1 hour at 425°—Gas 7. (Serve 2–3)

Almonds and Marrows is equally good eaten hot or cold. If served cold, cut into thick slices, arrange on a platter, surround with an alternation of **cucumber rounds** and **sweet-sour tomato slices** (slices of tomato soaked in **wine vinegar** and **brown sugar**).

STRAWBERRY SHERBERT

Fruit sherbets have been refreshing the parched throats of the heat-prostrated for centuries. A contrast beloved of Persian poets is the fire that is kindled by the glance of some dark-eyed beauty and the soothing ambrosia-like qualities of a sherbet cooled in mountain snow. An extravagant and ambrosia-like drink it certainly is, especially welcome on a sultry day, or simply when strawberries are cheap and plentiful.

Crush **1 lb. strawberries** thoroughly in a deep bowl. Add **3 slices seeded lemon, 1 tsp. orange flower essence, 2 cups cold water.** Mix together, cover, let stand about 3 hours. Then strain the mixture through a double layer of butter muslin, squeezing very well, so that every drop of liquid is extracted from the pulp. Stir in **½ lb. sugar** till it dissolves, strain through the muslin again. Put the resulting sherbet into a suitable utensil, cover, chill in the refrigerator till as cold as possible, or, better still, till a thin layer of ice has formed on top, then serve for drinking, or sipping, rather.

Israel

The Israel landscape is as striking in its variety as in its ex-
tremes of contrast. There are austere sun-bleached deserts
which yield to plains of a rich lush green. There is the tortured
heat of Sdom—1,286 feet below sea level, the lowest spot on
earth—and the pleasant coolness over the hills of Jerusalem.
There are cities of brash modernity and also many villages,
with cobbled streets winding off in all directions, set amid the
olive groves as in ancient times. The people are as richly varied
as the setting, and they have brought with them traditions of
cooking from nearly every corner of the world—Turkey, Iraq,
Cochin, India, Russia, Poland, France, America.

FELAFFEL

Felaffel, which arrived in Israel with the oriental influence, has
since become a national favourite, eaten in the streets at
practically any time of the day or night. The dispenser of this
savoury, the felaffel seller—with his pans of boiling oil, felaffel
paste, stacks of *pita* (yeasted flat bread), hot sauces and pickled
cucumbers—is held only slightly less high in the national
esteem. He listens to your order, always impatiently, and before
you've finished speaking he has deftly inserted felaffel between
the split *pita* and handed it to you. Never mind, there are
always so many other people waiting to be served . . .

Soak ½ **lb. dried chick peas** overnight or longer in plenty
of water to cover. Add ½ **tsp. bicarbonate of soda.** (The peas
should be soft enough to grind in a mortar or put through a
fine mincer without too much effort.) After soaking, rinse,

drain, and remove the transparent skins which slide off easily.

Grind or mince the peas as fine as possible and put into a deep bowl. Combine with 1¼ **tsp. coriander powder, 1 tbs. sea-salt** (or to taste), **3 crushed garlic cloves, 2 tbs. fine chopped sweet green pepper,** ¼ **tsp. chilli powder** (optional). Blend well.

Form lightly into balls the size of large marbles, deep fry in very hot **peanut oil** till brown and crisp. Drain on absorbent paper and serve, stuffed generously into split *pita* (often available in Greek provision stores), or sandwich-style in a folded over flap of white bread. (Enough for 4)

Accompany with varieties of **pickled vegetables, green salad, hot chilli peppers** or **Felaffel Hot Sauce.**

FELAFFEL HOT SAUCE

Blanch **4 medium size tomatoes** in freshly boiled water, peel, core, and put through a fine mincer. Add **1 tbs. lemon juice, 4–5 crushed cloves of garlic, 2 tsp. sea-salt, 2 tsp. fine minced parsley, 1 tsp. demerara sugar,** ½ **tsp. chilli powder.**

Bring to a light boil in a small heavy saucepan, then simmer for ½ hour uncovered. Remove from heat, allow to cool somewhat, add in another tbs. **lemon juice.** Cool completely.

An excellent dip for any fritter, and a very "hot" relish which goes a long way.

AVOCADOS

In years past the avocados one saw in the shops were objects of regal solitude. Then the Israelis adopted them, grew them, and made such a flourishing market out of them that other countries took notice and followed suit. Today the varieties one sees, practically all the year round, have so many origins it is hard to keep up with them. Pear-shaped and globe-shaped, smooth-skinned and crinkly, dark green and dark purple . . . all with subtle differences of taste, but with quality invariably excellent.

See also p. 11, then note a few more ways of filling and serving avocado halves:

With plain salad dressings; with **lemon juice, salt** and **olive oil;** with seasoned **sour cream** or **yoghourt;** with a selection of **chopped raw vegetables** moistened with **mayonnaise** or **dressing.**

AVOCADO VEGETABLE SALAD

Peel **2 medium sized avocados,** ripe but still firm. Cut lengthwise down the centres, remove stones. Now cut crosswise at ½-inch intervals to produce horse-shoe shaped wedges. Divide wedges into halves. Mix carefully with slices of **ripe tomato, cucumber,** and **2 hard-boiled eggs** cut in quarters. Cover with a light dressing of **Skordalia** (p. 135). Serve over beds of crisp **lettuce leaves.** (4)

AVOCADO FRUIT SALAD

Both of these salads could, appropriately, be called "health" salads, since avocados, besides being very light and digestible, are rich in vitamins and minerals. With the admixture of what follows here, the combination becomes particularly healthful.

For each portion, over a bed of wide-shredded **lettuce leaves,** arrange the following:

1 oz. stoned dates—sliced thin
½ **packet Philadelphia cream cheese**—cut into cubes
⅓ **sweet orange**—peeled, then cut into ¼-inch rounds
½ **medium size ripe avocado**—peeled and cut into chunks

Sprinkle over with **1 tbs. crushed walnuts,** then with 1½ **tbs.** of this dressing:

4 tbs. good quality salad cream
2 tbs. fresh lemon juice
2 tsp. demerara sugar
¼ **tsp. cardamom powder**

Enough dressing for 4 portions.

AVOCADO OMELETTE

For each serving: **4 oz. avocado flesh,** ripe or overripe—approximately half a medium size avocado—reduced to purée. Then added, together with ¾ **tsp. sea-salt,** to **2 beaten eggs.** Continue beating till smooth and frothy, and cook as for plain omelette in a lightly oiled pan. Let underside get golden, turn, and cook for a further minute only. Slide out on to a hot plate, sprinkle with fresh chopped **dill** or **parsley** and **lemon juice,** or serve with **lemon wedges.**

Very light and delicately flavoured.

VEGETABLE SHMALTZ

Anyone going through these pages will soon become aware of how many times reference is made to a shortening with the unwieldy name of *vegetable shmaltz*. If any apology is owing, it must be set against the sheer versatility of the substance. Because vegetable shmaltz is indispensable for preparing all sorts of savoury dishes and flavouring soups. It is extremely simple to make and will keep practically for ever. To produce a superior kind of shmaltz, however, it is worthwhile using a very good quality of Provençal olive oil.

Pour **1 cup olive oil** into a heavy frying pan (stainless steel is best). Heat to the boiling point, then add ¾ **of a large Spanish onion,** thinly sliced. Reduce heat to barely simmering and continue cooking gently till the onions turn golden brown (about 15–20 minutes). Remove pan from heat, transfer onions to a sheet of absorbent paper, pour oil through a double layer of butter muslin into a glass jar. When cool, cap down and keep in the refrigerator.

Vegetable shmaltz is absolutely delicious just spread over bread and sprinkled with salt. A spoonful or more added to plain mashed potatoes gives an instant richness of extra flavour. For a tasty Spring Vegetable Soup, merely combine some fine chopped vegetables with an appropriate amount of water, seasoning, and a tbs. or so of vegetable shmaltz. Bring to the boil, simmer for 20 minutes, serve immediately.

The fried onions, *greeben*, have a candy-like consistency and taste, due to their slow browning. They are also excellent added to mashed potatoes, eaten over bread and butter, or mixed with minced hard-boiled eggs.

According to Daniel-Rops, very great quantities of onions were grown in ancient Israel. And ever since, seemingly, the plant has played a supremely important role in the Jewish kitchen—in fact, there are very few cooked savouries without it. Perhaps second in popularity to onions are cucumbers, which in early Israel "were so much esteemed that whole fields were grown, fields that had to be guarded against the jackals who also appreciated cucumbers".*

* *Daily Life in Palestine at the Time of Christ.* Weidenfeld and Nicolson, 1962.

CUCUMBERS AND ALMONDS

Cut **1 large long cucumber** into 4-inch sections—it will probably make three such sections. Leave peel on, hollow out centres all the way through, allowing enough room for a generous amount of stuffing:

Macerate **1 green or red dried chilli pepper** in a mortar together with **1 tsp. sea-salt.** Add a **crushed clove of garlic, 1 oz. minced onion.** Grind together well. Then **2 oz. blanched almonds,** pulverized in the electric grinder, and **½ tsp. poppy seed.** Pound and mix to a sticky creamy mass.

Stuff into the hollowed cucumbers, stuffing in as much as possible. Put **1 tbs. olive oil** in a casserole, arrange the cucumbers snugly in. Surround with **4 medium size tomatoes** cut into eighths, sprinkle them over lightly with **sugar** and a good squeeze of **lemon juice.** Add several cut leaves of **fresh mint** over the tomatoes. Drizzle everything over with **olive oil,** then pour in **4 tbs. buttermilk.** Cover. Bake in a moderate oven (375°—Gas 5) for 1–1¼ hrs. Baste from time to time. Serve hot or cold with **dry-cooked rice.** (3–4)

QUICK PICKLED CARROTS

Make up a marinade of the following: **2 tbs. cider vinegar, ¼ cup water, ½ bay-leaf, 1 whole clove, 2 whole peppercorns, ⅛ tsp. crushed coriander seed, ¾ tsp. sea-salt, 1 tsp. soft light-brown sugar.** Pour into a narrow glass jar.

Add to it **¼ cup thin-sliced Spanish onion rings** and **3 medium size sweet carrots** sliced into paper thin rounds. Press cut vegetables below the surface of the marinade, allow to stand for 6 hours in a cool spot before using.

POTATO LATKES

When the festival of Hanukkah comes round, Israelis and Jews everywhere celebrate by making a form of potato fritter called *latke* which is deep-fried in oil. Hanukkah commemorates the victory of Judas Maccabeus over the Seleucids of the 2nd Century B.C. If anyone wonders what potatoes have to do with this, the answer is—it isn't the potato, but the oil which has symbolic meaning. And that, one supposes, is how traditions begin. *Latkes*, when they are correctly made, are crisp, light and dry—never oily.

Grate **1 lb. peeled potatoes** very fine. Then, most important, squeeze out all the liquid possible. What remains

d be an almost dry, fluffy white mass. Place it in a mixing
and add to it **1 large well-beaten egg, 1½ tsp. sea-salt,**
ch of **pepper, 3 tbs. matzo meal.** (Flour can be sub-
ed, but only matzo meal will ensure a light, airy texture.)
Blend all ingredients together very well.

Drop the *latke* mixture, by spoonfuls, into deep hot **oil** and
fry till all sides are golden brown. Drain immediately on
absorbent paper. Serve very hot, with separate bowls of **cold
sour cream** or **cold applesauce** for dipping. (4)

Variation: Griddle latkes Prepare *latke* mixture as above, drop by
spoonfuls on to a medium-hot griddle, lightly oiled with
vegetable shmaltz. Press each down with the back of a
spatula to make them thin. Fry both sides to light brown.
Serve with **cold applesauce.**

Jaffa is one of the oldest port cities in the world, known to
ancient Greece as Joppa. Legend has it that it was here, in
the harbour, that Andromeda was chained to her black rock
until the timely arrival of Perseus. In biblical days, the King of
Tyre proposed floating cedars from Lebanon to Jaffa for the
building of Solomon's Temple. It is still a notable town, with
narrow streets and picturesque markets, and a reputation for
exotic cooking. Here Israelis from Morocco, Tunisia, Egypt and
Yemen prepare and serve their traditional fare.

SALATA MECHOUIA

A very delicious Tunisian relish that is just as good eaten
with plain bread and butter as with Soft-Fried Matzo or
Moroccan Potatoes (see below).

Begin by having **6 medium size ripe tomatoes, 2 medium size sweet green peppers,** and several **lemons.**

Wash the green peppers, cut into halves, remove seeds, core
and pith. Put to boil in plenty of water. After 10 minutes, add
the tomatoes. Simmer a further 5–7 minutes, or till tomatoes
and peppers are really tender. Take from water and drain.

When tomatoes are cool enough to handle, remove cores and
skins. Then, holding each in the cup of the hand under cold
running water, squeeze gently from the bottom—to expel as
many seeds as possible. We have seen Tunisian ladies doing
this and they do it most expertly—the seeds rise up and float
away easily. Now cut the tomatoes into small pieces. Likewise,

cut the peppers into small pieces. Put both to drain in a large sieve for at least ½ hour (to allow most of the water to trickle away).

Place the drained vegetables on a large plate or chopping board and, wielding a sharp knife in either hand, use light slicing movements to mince fairly fine. Now add **1 crushed garlic clove,** the juice of **2 lemons, 2 tsp. sea-salt, 5 tbs. olive oil.** Blend well, then re-commence the slicing till the mixture is quite smooth. Taste and adjust seasoning if necessary. There should be a pronounced lemony flavour, so even more lemon juice may be needed. (4)

MOROCCAN POTATOES

We are poor people, we do not buy or sell,
our poverty maintains us.

(Old Moroccan Jewish saying)

Boil **1½–2 lb. potatoes** till nearly tender. Peel and cut into large cubes.

Put **2 tbs. olive oil** in a large heavy pan, add **2 chopped, spring onions, 2 crushed garlic cloves.** Fry lightly, stirring, till garlic is just beginning to colour, then add the potatoes, **1 tsp. crushed coriander seed, 1 tsp. sea-salt** (or to taste), and about **15 stoned black olives,** cut into halves.

Stir through and fry over a gentle heat until the olives are turning crisp and dry (about 15–20 minutes). Drizzle over with **1 tbs. soy sauce,** shake the pan to distribute, serve hot. (4–6)

CUMMIN CHEESE CAKES

Beat **¼ lb. dry cottage** or **curd cheese** with a little **cream.** Add salt to taste and form into little cakes. Sprinkle the tops with **cummin seed,** then press seeds in just below the surface. Leave to stand for an hour. Serve over **lettuce leaves** together with **sliced cucumbers, tomatoes** and **radishes,** swirled over with **sour cream.** (3)

BATINJAAN SPREAD

Wash **1 medium size aubergine (8 oz.)** and cut crosswise into ½-inch slices. Salt liberally, press under a weight in a sieve for an hour, pat dry.

Dip the slices in **matzo meal** (or **flour**) and fry in a little **olive oil** till golden on both sides. Drain on absorbent paper, remove skins.

Add a little more oil to the pan and fry a **small chopped onion (2 oz.)** till brown. Drain.

On a chopping board chop the onion and aubergine slices till you get a smooth creamy mass. While chopping add 1½ **tsp. sea-salt,** a pinch of fresh ground **black pepper, 2 tsp. wine vinegar.**

Chill and serve as a spread over **hot toast, plain buttered rye bread,** or buttered **crisp matzo.**

FESTIVE LADIES

These aromatic dumplings, so-named because of their carrot hats with sprigs of parsley in them, make a delightful meal for any festive occasion. The ingredients they contain are many, but the actual preparation is simple.

Pulverize **4 oz. almonds** in the electric grinder and transfer to a deep bowl. Then add

4 oz. courgettes—washed but not peeled, the ends cut off, grated fine and the juice squeezed out
1 medium carrot (2½–3 oz.)—grated fine, lightly squeezed out
½-inch slice fresh ginger—crushed through the garlic press
2½ oz. grated mild onion, together with its juice
2 large crushed cloves of garlic
1 tbs. grated celery—squeezed out
2½ tsp. sea-salt
½ tsp. demerara sugar
⅛ tsp. white pepper
a scant ¼ **tsp. turmeric**
2 medium size eggs
2½ oz. matzo meal

Mix everything together thoroughly.

In a deep large saucepan bring 1¾ **pints water** to the boil, along with: **1 celery stalk,** cut in thin slices, **1 carrot** cut into thin rounds, **1 small onion** cut into rings, **1 garlic clove** cut in half, **1 tbs. sea-salt,** ¾ **tsp. mixed pickling spice, 1 bay-leaf,** crumbled.

When the water is at a rolling boil, wet your hands with cold water and lightly form the almond/vegetable mixture into round shapes, the size of ordinary plums. As each is formed, slide it carefully into the boiling stock, wet your hands again (if necessary), and continue the process. As the saucepan begins to fill up, jiggle it slightly from time to time, to allow each

Festive Lady room to swell. When all the dumplings are in the pot, turn heat down to simmer, cover, and let cook for 35 minutes.

Allow to cool a little before removing the finished dumplings, very carefully, to a large platter. Decorate each with a slice of **cooked carrot,** pierce through with a tiny sprig of **parsley.** Let get completely cold before serving over **crisp lettuce,** together with **rye bread and butter** and **Khrain.** (Enough for 6)

If you like, strain the remaining stock through butter muslin, return to the pot, add Agar Agar (proportion: ½ **tsp. Agar to 1 cup stock**). Bring to a light boil, simmer gently for a minute, cool, allow to jell. Serve portions of the jellied stock with the Festive Ladies.

KHRAIN

This ruby-coloured relish is a development of plain horseradish, but more tangy and refreshing and a little less sharp. A small serving of it is complementary to Festive Ladies, or Soft-Fried Matzo, or most anything savoury.

Grate (near an open window—from which draw healing draughts of fresh air) **4 oz. peeled fresh horseradish.** Grate very fine.

Add to it **2 oz. raw fresh beetroot,** also peeled and grated very fine, **2 tsp. demerara sugar,** the juice of **1 medium sized lemon.** Blend together very well and store in a tightly covered glass jar. The best size jar is one where the *khrain* comes to the top. Otherwise, see that the mixture is below the liquid level, by pressing it under if necessary. Keep in refrigerator.

SABBATH PEPPERS

Parboil **4 medium size, well-shaped, sweet green peppers** for 3–4 minutes. Drain, cool, and prepare a stuffing:

2 oz. walnuts—pulverized in the electric grinder
8 tbs. matzo meal
4 tbs. plain flour
4 tbs. dry bread-crumbs (untoasted)
5-6 tbs. vegetable shmaltz
1 tbs. sea-salt
3 oz. mild onion—chopped and fried golden in olive oil

Mix well together.
Slice tops off peppers, just under the stalks. Scoop out seeds

and pith, being careful not to cut through the sides or bottoms. Fill with the stuffing mixture, packing down well. Drizzle over with more vegetable shmaltz, replace pepper caps.

Warm **1 tbs. vegetable shmaltz** in a medium sized earthenware casserole. Arrange peppers in upright. Surround with **3-4 rough cut tomatoes,** lightly sugared and salted. Cover, bake at 350° (Gas 4) for 45 minutes to 1 hour, till stuffing is cooked through. Uncover casserole for the last 10 minutes. Serve with plenty of **salad.** (4)

SOFT-FRIED MATZO

The unleavened crisp bread called *matzo* is eaten traditionally during Passover, but is available at most grocers the year round. It is a delicious and useful accompaniment to savouries and soups, and makes an interesting change from toast with morning tea or coffee—just butter and salt it—or a base for almost any kind of spread. Treated in the manner following, it is a light yet sustaining luncheon, especially good with mixed salad, or sliced dill-pickled cucumber and ripe tomato, and a glass of sherry.

For each portion, break **2 matzo squares** into small pieces in a shallow bowl. Cover with **cold water,** for no longer than 45 seconds to 1 minute, then quickly drain and press out.

Add **1 well-beaten egg** and ½ **tsp. sea-salt.** Mix matzo and egg together thoroughly.

Heat 1½ **tbs. olive oil** in a medium sized frying pan. Pour in egg/matzo mixture and quickly spread it out with the back of a spoon or fork, so that it covers most if not all of the pan bottom. Let it cook over a fairly brisk heat till the underside is golden, then turn and complete the other side.

POTATO FRUIT CAKES

A dish to celebrate the harvest.

Steep **6 dried prunes** in freshly boiled water for 10 minutes. Drain, pit and mince fine.

Boil **1 lb. potatoes** till soft. Drain and steam in the pot for a few minutes to dry thoroughly. Peel and mash very smooth. When cool add: **1 beaten egg,** ⅛ **tsp. powdered ginger,** ½ **tsp. soft light-brown sugar, 1 scant tsp. sea-salt, 3 tbs. matzo meal** (or enough to make a pliable dough). Mix everything very well and divide into 4 equal parts. Form into spheres.

Heat 1½ **tbs. vegetable shmaltz** in a small pan. Fry **3 oz.**

chopped Spanish onion till it begins to brown. Add **2 crushed garlic cloves** (optional) and fry a further 2 minutes. Now add **7 oz. tart apple,** peeled and sliced thin, **¼ tsp. sea-salt, 1 tsp. soft light-brown sugar,** and the minced prunes. Stir through, cover, simmer gently till the apple falls apart. When removing cover, shake away the accumulated moisture. Mash mixture lightly with a fork. Add **1½ tbs. matzo meal,** stir through again, let cook another 2 minutes, uncovered. Remove from heat.

On a pastry board, well-sprinkled with matzo meal, roll potato spheres lightly out into rounds about 5 inches wide.

Spoon 2–3 tbs. of the apple/onion mixture along the centres of each, fold over into half-moon shapes, press edges down well to seal. Arrange on a lightly oiled baking sheet, brush tops of potato cakes with beaten **egg yolk,** bake in a moderate oven (350–375°—Gas 4–5) for ½ hour, or till tops are crisp and light brown. (Serves 4)

POMERANTZEN

Valuable experiments are being carried on in many parts of the world to discover how plant products can provide plentiful amounts of cheap and highly nutritious food. In Israel, this work derives from the late Dr. Weizmann, its first President. It is said that, in his attempts to extract protein from plants, Dr. Weizmann evolved "steaks" out of orange peel, which his unknowing guests used to eat as the "real thing". As the method is still in its infancy it cannot, unfortunately, be given here. Instead, here is a straightforward way of preparing orange peel, as a sweet particularly loved by children.

Choose **3–4 oranges,** large and thick-skinned, Jaffa prefer-ably. With a sharp knife, carefully pare away the very thin outer layer of the peel (zest). Cut oranges into quarters, remove orange flesh, leave pith intact. Cut quartered peels into inch wide sections (use orange flesh for fruit salads).

Simmer peels in plenty of water for 15 minutes, then drain.

In a saucepan, boil **1 cup water** with **2½ cups castor sugar** till liquid threads from the end of a spoon (approximately 30 minutes). Then put the peels in and simmer gently for about an hour—they should be quite translucent by this time. Drain well and roll immediately in **powdered sugar.** Let them dry and cool on a rack before storing in a paper-lined tin.

* * *

Most peoples with a mythology have traditions of a golden age, at which time animals were regarded as *elder brothers, younger brothers, cousins, the other people,* and even as *gods.* But few peoples have ever thought of the animals as *teachers.* Yet a reference in the Talmud cites this instance: "If the Torah (first five books of the Bible) had not been given, we could have learned modesty from the cat, honesty from the ant, chastity and good manners [from other creatures] . . ."—*'Erubin 100 B (Talmud)*

From no particular land

"*Tortillina* corn powder" is based on an Indian preparation of the Americas—an adaptation of maize flour widely used for the flatbread known as *tortillas*.

Where peoples live close to one another not only friendships but food habits may be exchanged. Here is a neighbourly fusion of Japanese-American with central American cooking, and traces of European added in.

TWO-WAY STICKY MAIZE SHAPES AND SEAWEED

Rinse very thoroughly **1 oz. Iziki seaweed** (see p. 17). Leave to soak in a pot of water for an hour, then drain or shake dry.

Mix together: **1 cup "Tortillina" powder (5 oz.), ¾ cup water, 1 small crushed garlic clove, 2 tsp. soy sauce** (Kikkoman), **½ tsp. sea-salt.** Blend to a soft sticky dough. Form into 3 large balls, let stand for 5 minutes. Then cut into small irregular shapes about an inch wide.

Heat **1 tbs. peanut oil** in a large heavy pan, add **1 tbs. Kikkoman.** As it begins to splutter pour in, immediately, **½ cup water.** Reduce heat, put in the maize shapes, a few at a time. Shake pan to prevent sticking, cover, simmer 5 minutes. Now turn shapes over with a spatula and separate if necessary, add **½ cup buttermilk** and **¼ cup water.** Shake pan again, cover, simmer 12–15 minutes. Stir frequently. Then empty pan contents into a bowl and keep warm.

Crush a sliver of **garlic** and a small slice of **fresh ginger** into a mortar. Blend to a smooth paste, then add **2 tbs. Kikkoman.** Amalgamate.

Reheat clean pan with a sprinkling of **peanut oil,** just enough to make an oily film, toss in the seaweed, stir, add soy sauce/ginger mixture and **¼ cup water,** stir again, bring to a simmer.

Now add half the quantity of maize shapes to the pan, along with about 3 tbs. of the buttermilk sauce. Shake pan, cover, cook gently 15 minutes more. Stir from time to time to prevent sticking.

Serve two-way maize shapes together with seaweed and buttermilk sauces over **dry-cooked rice.** (4–6)

ASH-BAKED POTATOES

Few foods are more evocative of childhood or youth, of indolent late summer afternoons spent watching the smoke rising from burning leaves, than potatoes baked in the embers of those leaves. When a good heap of autumn leaves is burning well, push large potatoes, washed but not peeled, deep into the glowing ash. Keep the fire going briskly, turn the potatoes occasionally with long broken-off branches, let the potatoes smoulder away as long as possible—about an hour and a half at least. Have your plates ready in the garden, split the potatoes open, butter, salt, and eat, skins included, after you have brushed them down.

Different leaves impart different flavours; chestnut is excellent and so is oak, but a combination of others should be quite as good.

SWEET-CORN SPINACH-SOUR

Wash ½ **lb. spinach** thoroughly, drain, discard tough stems, chop coarsely.

Heat 1½ **tbs. olive oil** in a large pan, fry **1 medium size onion** sliced into rings. Fry till golden and almost crisp.

In a cup blend 1½ **tbs. wine vinegar, 1 tbs. water, 2 tsp. demerara sugar, ½–¾ tsp. sea-salt, 6 stoned bland black olives,** minced.

Pour over the frying onions, stir, and simmer a minute or two. Add spinach, **2 tomatoes (4 oz.),** peeled, cored, seeded and mashed with a fork, **2 tbs. tinned sweet-corn kernels.** Stir again, cover pan, simmer 15 minutes or till spinach is completely tender. (2)

CAULIFLOWER AND GESKA SAUCE

Grate the flowerets of ½ **medium size cauliflower.** Grate fine. Fry a few minutes over a low heat in **1 tbs. peanut oil,** add **a crushed clove of garlic** and **sea-salt** to taste. Stir through. Reduce heat to a gentle simmer, cover pan, cook 15 minutes, adding a little water from time to time. Then sprinkle in **2 tbs. fine grated Geska cheese,** continue simmering another 3 minutes.

An excellent sauce for pouring over boiled or steamed vegetables—**potatoes, green beans, carrots, peas.** (Serves 3–4)

AVOCADO CHILLI DIP

Mash the flesh of **2 ripe or overripe medium size avocados,** add immediately **2–3 tbs. lemon juice.** Blend well. Mix in with **1 large, peeled ripe tomato,** chopped fine, **1 small, minced celery stalk, 1 fine-minced, seeded green chilli pepper, 1 tsp. sea-salt, 2 tbs. plain yoghourt.** Whip till light and creamy. Chill.

Pile in a bowl, decorate with strips of **sweet green and red pepper.** Use as a dip for chunks of bread or toast, or as an appetizer. (6–8)

BUCKWHEAT AND BOWKNOTS

In **1½ tbs. vegetable shmaltz** fry **4 oz. thin-sliced onion rings** till golden. Remove from pan to bowl. Wipe pan clean.

Dry-fry **4 oz. (½ cup) buckwheat groats** (kasha) for 5–7 minutes, stirring occasionally. Then add **1¼ cups water,** cover the pan, cook gently till liquid absorbs. Test grains for tenderness—if not completely tender, add a few drops water more. Then add **1 tsp. sea-salt, 2 tbs. vegetable shmaltz** and stir through. Remove from pan to bowl containing onions. Keep warm.

Cook **9 oz. bowknot-shaped pasta** in plenty of boiling salted water. Cook till tender. Drain very thoroughly, add **1–1½ tbs. butter** and **1 scant tsp. sea-salt.** When butter melts, add bowknots to buckwheat and onions. Mix through. Serve with a **green salad** and a chilled white wine. (4–5)

BEAN SPROUTS MATZO FRITTERS
(DRAGONS' BEARDS)

Break **3 squares of matzo** into small pieces, soak for 1 minute in cold water. Drain, press dry, place in a bowl. Add in **2 beaten eggs, 1 chopped stalk celery, 2 tbs. minced sweet pepper** (red or green), **2 minced spring onions, ½ cup bean sprouts** (tinned or fresh—if tinned, drain very well), **1 tbs. soy sauce, sea-salt,** a small piece of **crushed fresh ginger.** Blend together.

Drop by large spoonfuls into very hot deep **oil.** Fry till both sides are golden. Drain on crumpled brown paper. Serve with small bowls of **soy sauce** for dipping. (4)

COURGETTES AND EGGS

India, Greece and Israel contribute to this harmoniously-spiced omelette.

Cut ½ **lb. courgettes** into ½-inch rounds, salt, let drain under a weight in a sieve for ½ hour. Pat dry. Heat **1 tbs. olive oil** in a fairly large pan. Fry **1½ oz. chopped onion** for 3 minutes, follow with ¼ **tsp. mustard seed** (black), ¼ **tsp. cummin seed,** a rounded ¼ **tsp. curry powder.** Fry and stir another minute, add the courgette rounds. Cover pan, continue cooking gently another 20–25 minutes, or till courgettes are tender.

Beat **2 eggs** together with **1 tbs. yoghourt, 1 small chopped and seeded chilli pepper, 1 tbs. matzo meal.** Pour over the vegetables, sprinkle with a little **chilli powder,** cover pan, let eggs set. Add a little more oil to the pan if necessary, jiggle to distribute well. Then turn omelette over, cook a few seconds more, turn out immediately on a heated platter. (3)

ALMOND BAKE

Prepare

6 oz. almonds—pulverize in electric grinder
½ **tsp. mixed pickling spice**—grind to powder in mortar
2–3 tbs. chopped onion—fry till golden in olive oil
a slice of crustless bread—soak in cold water and squeeze out

Put the ground almonds into a bowl. Add **1 tsp. sea-salt,** the powdered pickling spice, the chopped fried onion, **1 egg,** the soaked bread, crumbled, **1½ tbs. matzo meal, 2 tbs. water.** Mix well together, making sure all the ingredients are thoroughly blended.

Line a small loaf tin with aluminium foil. Oil it. Then pile the almond mixture into it smoothly. Bake (at 400°—Gas 6) for 35–40 minutes, or till the top is rich golden. Turn out on a rack and allow to cool. Peel away the foil. Cut in thick slices. Very good with any raw salad. (4)

FLAKED CEREALS

The whole grains of cereals are very rich in protein and minerals. Flaked whole cereals are available at most health food stores and specialty shops. In this form they are particularly digestible and delicious, and an entire meal can be based on them and cooked within 15 minutes.

Flaked Millet Fry   Heat **1 tbs. olive oil** in a large heavy pan. Add **2 cups flaked millet.** Stir through and fry on a low heat for 5 minutes, stirring occasionally. In the meantime, prepare your fresh vegetables:

> **1 celery stalk**—chopped fine
> **1 small carrot**—grated
> **2 spring onions**—chopped fine
> **1 tomato, unpeeled**—cut in small pieces

Add about 1½ **cups water** to the millet and stir till the grain is well moistened—*not wet*. Add prepared vegetables and 1½ **tsp. sea-salt** and distribute through. Press millet down lightly and fairly evenly. Turn heat up to medium and cook till underside is golden and lightly crisp—5–7 minutes. Sprinkle over with **Goma Sio** (p. 97) or **soy sauce** and serve. (3–4)

Note: There are other flaked whole cereals besides millet—rice, maize, rye, barley—which can be combined with one another in cereal frys. A basically good combination is, however, 1½ cups millet to ½ cup of any other.

ONION-NOODLE OMELETTE

Cook **4 oz. noodles** in plenty of boiling salted water till tender. Drain well, add **1 tsp. olive oil** and ½ **tsp. sea-salt.** Mix through, cover, keep warm.

Heat a combination of 1½ **tbs. olive oil** and **butter** in a large heavy pan. Add **2 oz. chopped sweet onion,** fry till golden and crisp. Add noodles, mix with onion, level off neatly.

Beat **4 eggs** together with ½ **tsp. sea-salt** and a pinch of **white pepper.** Pour over the noodles, cover pan, let eggs set well. When bottom is golden, loosen edges all round with a spatula, invert omelette out on a large plate. Then slide it back into the pan, uncooked side downward, cook a further minute or two. Cut into pie-shaped wedges, sprinkle with **chopped fresh parsley,** serve on heated plates. (3–4)

PEACH FOAM

When **peaches** are most plentiful and at their cheapest, peel a half dozen of them and cut into small pieces, then mash them

with a silver fork. Put the peach mass into a bowl, add about
½ **cup fine sugar** (or to taste). Beat well with the same silver
fork, then add the **white of an egg** already beaten very stiff.
Blend through till mixture is light and foamy. Chill. Serve
topped with **crushed toasted nuts—pistachios** preferably.
(4)

MABELETTES

Why these are called *Mabelettes* we can't remember. But we
think there used to be a girl called Mabel who made them.
(Mabel, wherever you are, thank you!)

Sift **3 oz. plain flour** into a bowl, together with a pinch
of **salt** and **1 rounded tsp. baking powder.** Burrow out the
usual dry well, break in **1 egg,** mix lightly. Then add, very
slowly and mixing constantly, ½ **cup milk** sweetened through
with **4 tbs. maple syrup.** Beat lightly till smooth and follow
with: **1 tbs. olive oil,** ⅛ **tsp. cardamom powder.** Blend
well and let stand 20 minutes or so.

Oil a griddle lightly, bring it up to a medium/brisk heat.
Ladle out Mabel's mixture in small or large spoonfuls. When
tops get somewhat dry and finely perforated turn over. Brown
undersides. But work quickly, as they get done quickly. Stack in
4s or 5s, sandwiching in between with **sour cream.** Sprinkle
over with more maple syrup if desired.

For children

Jack be nimble, Jack be quick,
Jack jump over the candlestick.

QUICK ENERGY BREAKFAST
A very stimulating way to begin the morning, either for children or for adults. Simple to make, refreshing to eat, healthful in all its properties.

For each serving, cut **1 crisp apple** (unpeeled but washed) into small cubes, or grate very fine. Sprinkle over with **lemon juice** and mix. Then add **1 tbs. chopped almonds,** a generous sweetening of **raw Barbados sugar,** or **honey,** and mix again. Blend with **2–3 tbs. plain yoghourt.**

HAPPY FACES LUNCHEON SALAD
Cover individual plates with a layer of crisp **lettuce leaves.** In the centre of each put a serving of **cottage cheese,** formed lightly into a round disc. Space **pineapple segments** all round the outer edges of the cheese. Make a face inside— **raisins** for the eyes, a **pimento-stuffed olive** for the nose, a strip of **red pepper** for the mouth, turned up in a smile (Or do it any other way your artistic fancy takes you.) Decorate lettuce with **chopped nuts,** diced cooked **beetroot,** grated **carrot,** swirl over with a little thin **salad cream.**

SWALLOWS' NESTS
For children with bird-like appetites?

Make up a batter: **6 oz. plain flour, 2 eggs, ½ cup milk, 2 tsp. sea-salt.** Beat lightly till fairly smooth. Let stand while you do the following:

Grate coarsely **2 oz. carrots,** cut **4 oz. peeled raw potatoes** into match-stick slivers.

Add potato and carrot to batter, mix through, drop by spoonfuls into deep hot **oil.** Fry till golden on all sides. Drain. Sprinkle with **sea-salt,** serve immediately with a raw **salad.** (4–5)

COTTAGE CHEESE POTATOES

An excellent way of balancing protein (cottage cheese) with alkaline-forming food (potato).

Bake **4 good-sized, scrubbed potatoes** in foil till tender (about 1–1¼ hours). Remove foil and allow to cool somewhat. Make a slit into the top of each potato, scoop out as much of the centres as you can without breaking them. Mix with: **½ cup cottage cheese, 1 tsp. chopped fresh parsley,** the juice of **half a small lemon, sea-salt, pepper, 2 chopped spring onions, ¼ tsp. paprika.** Pile mixture back into potato shells, top with sprigs of **parsley.** Serve with **cucumber slices** blended with **yoghourt.** (4)

COTTAGE CHEESE LUNCHEONS

Other nourishing luncheons can be made quickly with raw vegetable combinations. With cauliflower, celery, carrots, radishes, minced fairly fine. With young green beans, tomato, tender leaves of watercress, cut rather coarsely. Mix cottage cheese with a little cream or yoghourt to soften if necessary, then blend with your choice of vegetables. Season with sea-salt, arrange over lettuce, top with spring onion strips. Accompany with lots of bread and butter.

NUT PUFFS

Pigeons, like humans, are capable of forming "complex concepts". So say American scientists who know both. Other investigators have been equally astonished to find that pigeons are capable of acting as "inspectors" on factory assembly lines, testing transistors. And some of them are so gifted they have been taught to spot forgeries on cheques. When observed in their natural state, pigeons exhibit distinct individual personalities, far removed from what we may think when seeing them *en masse* in Trafalgar Square. Although we cannot speak for all of them, those that assemble at our kitchen window find Nut Puffs a very flavoury delicacy—and children usually do the same.

Pulverize **3 oz. almonds** through your electric grinder. Put in a bowl.

Add **1 medium size egg, an inch-thick slice of crustless bread** soaked for 3 minutes in water, then squeezed out and crumbled, **1½ tsp. sea-salt,** a good pinch of **dry crumbled dill.** Mix together to form a soft dough.

Put a little **flour** in a plate, dust your palms with it. Take up spoonfuls of the almond mixture and form lightly into small barrel shapes. Fry in deep hot **oil** until richly brown on all sides. Drain. Serve hot or cold. (4–5)
Very tasty with Many-Coloured Rice Salad.

MANY-COLOURED RICE SALAD

Make up **1¾ cups dry-cooked rice** (from ¾ cup raw), with a small pinch of **saffron** added to the cooking water. Let rice cool, transfer to a deep bowl, mix in with small amounts of **chopped sweet red pepper, celery, spring onion; sliced raw button mushrooms, rough-cut tomatoes, minced parsley; chopped nuts** and **seedless raisins.** Moisten with a little **olive oil,** just enough to make the rice grains glisten, season with **sea-salt, lemon juice,** a dusting of **sugar.** Toss well. (4)

POACHED EGG SPECIAL

A very simple way of enticing a child's appetite, and one that provides good amounts of iron and vitamin B complex.

Make up a portion of **Green Simmer** (p. 21). Prepare **poached eggs** as you like them. Serve eggs over Simmer, surround with **buttered toast fingers.**

FRUITY SOUP

Clean **8 oz. strawberries,** press through a fine sieve into a saucepan. Grate **2 medium size eating apples,** peel, core and all. Add to the saucepan together with **1¼ cups sweet white grape juice,** ¼ **tsp. grated lemon rind, 2 tbs. demerara sugar** (or thereabouts). Bring to a light boil, then simmer gently for 15 minutes. Pass through the sieve, discard residue, return mixture to the saucepan and the heat. Add in **1 tsp. cornflour** dissolved in **1 tbs. of grape juice.** Stirring constantly, simmer 3 minutes more. Cool. Chill. (4)

CHIMPANZEES' DELIGHT

"The origins of music and dancing are to be found very deep in the human past . . . a certain sense of rhythm can be observed in some of the great apes, especially the chimpanzees. Both in freedom and captivity competent observers have often seen chimpanzees performing a childish round while holding hands. Sometimes these rounds are directed 'by a sort of master of ceremonies who leads the dance by clapping his hands and striking his feet on the earth. Sometimes, too, the females dress themselves up for these dances with lianas and leaves."*

Not only dancing but fruit-picking is a favourite pastime of chimpanzees in their natural surroundings. A fruit eating orgy can go on for hours with many exchanges of good-humoured banter. The salad that follows, although it is not, strictly speaking, in the "jungle" class, makes an acceptable substitute for urban-living chimpanzees—and most children. Try it next time your child gives his whole fruit that very "absent" look.

Into a bowl
> cut **2 ripe bananas** in rounds
> and **2 crisp apples** in cubes
> cut in small pieces of **dried apricot**
> add a handful of **halved seedless grapes,** or **whole raisins**
> the **juice of an orange**
> a squirt of **lemon juice**
> blend with a nice amount of **soft light-brown sugar**
> stir in a goodly portion of **yoghourt**
> top with **crushed nuts,** preferably **almonds**

Enough for 3–4 small children, or one full grown chimpanzee.

TAPIOCA GRAPE JELL

A tapioca pudding with "mystery" to it.

Bring to a light boil in a saucepan **1 cup water, ½ cup sweet purple grape juice,** together with **5–6 tbs. demerara sugar** (or to taste). Stir till sugar dissolves, then simmer. Sprinkle in **6 tbs. quick-cooking tapioca** (*Groult* brand is excellent and widely available). Stirring continuously, simmer 5–7 minutes more, till tapioca looks transparent. Remove pan from heat, add **1 tsp. lemon juice,** stir, pour into small glass bowls. After a few minutes, when it has jelled slightly, top with a light snowfall of **fine grated lemon rind.** Chill before serving. (4–6)

MINIATURE DOUGHNUTS

These delightful tiny pastry rings, almost dry on the outside, oozing with juices from within, should please almost anyone.

Sieve **1 cup plain flour** into a bowl together with **¼ tsp. bicarbonate of soda.** Mix to a soft dough with **½ cup sour**

* From *Man in Search of his Ancestors*, by André Senet—Allen & Unwin, 1955.

cream. Knead for a few minutes on a floured board, adding a tiny bit more flour only if necessary.

Heat deep **oil** in a saucepan. Prepare a small amount of **cinnamon** and **pulverized demerara sugar.** Have a small bowl of **maple syrup** standing by.

With floured palms, pinch off very small bits of the dough, roll between the hands into thick pencil shapes, pinch the ends together to form small doughnuts. Drop into the hot oil, fry till rich brown on both sides. Remove from oil with a fork, shake excess oil off lightly, dip immediately into the maple syrup— see that both sides receive the liquid. (If you listen close, you will hear the hot doughnuts sizzle as they absorb the syrup.) Remove from maple syrup after a few minutes—or give your child this job—set on a plate, sprinkle over with the cinnamon/ fine sugar. Eat when cold, or nearly cold.

(Hard to judge the amount produced since they were eaten so quickly.)

MAPLE SAUCE

Simmer $1\frac{1}{2}$ **cups maple syrup** for 5–7 minutes. Add in $\frac{1}{4}$ **cup chopped nuts (pecans** or **almonds),** continue simmering— and stirring—a few minutes longer. Remove from heat. Cool.

Use the nut-indoctrinated sauce over **plain ice cream, rice puddings, pancakes.**

RAW FRUIT TARTS
Found your mittens you lovely kittens?
Then you shall have some pie . . .

Use **Ice-box cookie dough** for this one (p. 124).

Have ready as many tart tins as are required. Slice a quantity of thin rounds of cookie dough. Leave them to soften a bit, then form lightly into small balls. Roll out into thin round discs, according to size of tart tins. Arrange in the tins, prick lightly over with a fork, bake in a moderate oven (375°—Gas 5) for 10–12 minutes or till pale biscuit in colour. Cool.

Fill pastry shells with **fresh fruit,** chopped and sweetened, or with **mashed bananas** flavoured with **maple syrup** and **lemon juice.** Sprinkle over with **crushed nuts.**

The indifference of children to meat is one
proof that the taste [for it] is unnatural . . .
Jean-Jacques Rousseau (*Emile*)

A few last words

Nothing affects men's ideas (and women's) so much as other men's ideas. This is practically a platitude, and examples are hardly necessary to point it up. All the same, it is interesting to know that the American Benjamin Franklin was first impelled to vegetarianism after reading the work of Thos. Tryon. And it was from reading Benjamin Franklin, as he tells us, that Franz Kafka as a young man felt the same urge to change. This might be regarded as a special case, however, since ideas which set out to influence settled customs and traditions—and what is more custom-bound and traditional than our habits of eating? —are usually resisted. This is very nicely caught in one of the Kai Lung stories* where a certain young man is asked, in terms of implied reproach, whether he is not the leader of a notorious band of local thieves. He replies: "My revered father was of that craft before me and his venerated sire likewise in turn. How then could I, without being unfilial to a criminal degree, [reject] what was good enough for them?" A very extreme example of "Chinese" ancestral habit carried to its ultimate and absurd logic?

If some of the recipes in this book have pleased you we shall be content. If they have aroused in you the possibility of changing your ancestral eating habits ... well, we can only hope.

SALLY AND LUCIAN BERG
London, 1966

* In *Kai Lung Unrolls His Mat*, by Ernest Bramah. Richards Press, 1942.

Menus

Eating is a necessity—eating imaginatively
is an art.

LA ROCHEFOUCAULD

There is no need to base your meals on one country's cooking exclusively. You can range, for example, from Spanish appetizers to Italian entrées to Near Eastern sweets. But try whenever possible to include raw vegetables or fruit with each cooked meal when planning your menus. This will make up for any vitamins or minerals lost in cooking.

Here is a selection of Luncheon, Dinner and Snack menus, some simple or light, others more elaborate and ample.

LUNCHEONS

(1) Burgers on toasted rolls, Cole Slaw (Special), soft drinks.
(2) Polish Luncheon Platter, rye bread and butter, fruit, yoghourt.
(3) Foil-Baked Potatoes, Antipasto, fruit, lemon tea.
(4) Any 2 or 3 Smörgåsbrod, lager.
(5) Avocado Fruit Salad, French bread, Raw Fruit Tarts, coffee.
(6) Mushroom Watercress Soup, Salade Niçoise, Tapioca Grape Jell.
(7) Poached Egg Special, Apple-Cinnamon Pancakes.
(8) Coriander Cheese Dip, Balkan Cucumber Salad, Quick Deep Strudel.
(9) Bread Salad, Chick Pea Scramble, sliced melon.
(10) Mixed Fritters, Salata Mechouia, halva.
(11) Mushroom-Walnut Pancakes, Fruited Cabbage Salad, Honey Pears.
(12) Lemon Soup, Red-Cooked Mushroom, tomato slices, fruit.
(13) Buckwheat and Bowknots, Mixed Salad, light red wine.
(14) Griddle Latkes, Summer Salad, fruit.
(15) Cottage Cheese Potatoes, Pickled Mushrooms, Date-Sugared Apples.

(16) Fruity Soup, Winter Rice Salad, almonds and halva.

(17) Flaked Millet Fry, fresh fruit, lemon tea.

(18) Apple Beets and sour cream, Salade Benvenuto, dry cider.

(19) Three Greens Boil, Dilled New Potatoes, bread and butter, ale.

(20) Marinated Green Beans, noodles and Gascon Sauce, Peach Foam.

(21) Mayflower Salad, hot French bread, Ice-Box Cookies, coffee.

(22) Spiced Gluten Kebab, Pickled Lettuce and Cucumber, fruit.

(23) Potato and Pois Mange Tout Salad, bread chunks, lime-blossom tisane.

(24) Mushroom Maize Casserole, lettuce salad, Little Clotted Cream Gateaux.

(25) Cauliflower and Potato Zharkoye, Quick Salted Cucumbers, fruit.

(26) Halushki and sour cream, Portuguese Salad II, lemon tea.

(27) Spicy Chick Pea Puffs, Coconut Rice, red wine.

(28) Bean Sprouts and Matzo Fritters, Sweet-Sour Radishes, jasmine tea.

(29) Boiled new potatoes with Skordalia, Salade Benvenuto, Raw Fruit Tarts.

(30) Avocado Vegetable Salad, bread and butter, Moorish Rice Cream.

(31) Courgettes Béarnaise, Potato Fruit Cakes, white wine.

(32) Samosas, Fried Rice II, chutneys, tea.

(33) Artichokes, Double-Dressed Potato Salad, grapes and halva.

(34) Yablonchiki Potatoes, lettuce salad, Dill-Pickled Cucumbers, fruit.

(35) Smetana Salad, rye bread, Cherry Dumplings.

(36) Nut Puffs, Chicory and Plum Salad, Hashmerim.

(37) Clear Mushroom Soup, Green Tomato Omelette, almonds and raisins.

(38) Aubergine Baby Omelettes with Tartare Sauce, Cole Slaw (Special), tea.

(39) Green Simmer, Sweet Corn Fritters, fresh cherries.

(40) Avocado Omelette, Portuguese Salad I, moselle.

(41) Red Pepper Pasta, Marinated Green Beans, Honey Pears.

(42) Cauliflower à la king on toast, Pickled Salad, Mabelettes.

(43) Cummin Cheese Cakes, Paula's Pickled Peppers, black and green olives, ripe tomato slices, fruit.

(44) Sliced Klops, Khrain, Dill-Pickled Cucumbers, beer.

(45) Noodles and Cheese, Mixed Salad, wine.

(46) Sweet-Corn Spinach-Sour, Dilled New Potatoes, apples and yoghourt.

(47) Courgettes (After Apicius), plain buttered noodles, tisane.

(48) Cottage Cheese and Onion Pizzas, Fennel Salad, Banana Maple.

(49) Soft-Fried Matzo, Flavoury Radishes, sherry, Chew-Strew.

(50) Cottage Cheese Luncheon, toasted bagels, Plain Country Fruit Bake.

DINNERS

(1) Salade Benvenuto, Gulyas Faludi, wine, Peach Foam.

(2) Pisto, Sesame Potatoes, Portuguese Salad II, fruit.

(3) "Much to Eat", Lemon Cucumbers, Anatolia Fruit Salad.

(4) Fried Gluten and Eggs, Summer Salad, Pomerantzen and almonds.

(5) Spiced Puris, Sour Dal, Punjabi Vegetable Curry, quick relishes.

(6) Pecan Layered Casserole, Cole Slaw (Special), Banana Maple.

(7) Instant Soup, Asparagus and Potatoes, Cranberry Sauerkraut, fresh fruit.

(8) Potato Latkes, Layered Salad, Maize Galettes, coffee.

(9) Lemon Soup, Lasagne, Mixed Salad, white wine.

(10) Im-Hasha, Peach-Almond Pancakes, wine.

(11) Pasta and Potatoes with Pesto Sauce, calamata olives, halva.

(12) Mushroom Watercress Soup, Basque Omelette, French bread, fruit.

(13) Artichokes and dressing, Foil-Baked Potatoes, Cherry Dumplings.

(14) Fruity Soup, The Imam's Moustache, Miniature Doughnuts, Turkish coffee.

(15) Union Suit Stew, rye bread chunks, cold ale.

(16) Skewered Vegetables, Dry-Cooked Rice, Salata Mech-ouia, fresh grapes.

(17) Sliced Melon, Green-Red Eggs, *grissini*, lettuce salad, chilled white wine.

(18) Avocado Chilli Dip, Pasta with Wine and Black Olive Sauce, cherries.

(19) Cucumbers and Almonds, Saffron Rice, Maize Galettes.

(20) Little Gem Grills, sliced Almond Bake, Chilled Stuffed Tomatoes, fresh lemonade.

(21) Baby Marrows Yahni Style, plain buttered noodles, yoghourt.

(22) Grapefruit, Mushroom Pâté, Festive Ladies with Khrain, sliced tomato and cucumber, lemon tea.

(23) Antipasto, Asparagus and Potatoes, dried apricots and hazelnuts, tea.

(24) Courgettes and Eggs, brown bread, lettuce salad, pomegranates.

(25) Grated Potato Pudding, Fruited Cabbage Salad, strawberries, coffee.

(26) Chilled Lemon Soup, Prunes and Potatoes, Shredded Celery-Lovage Appetizer, tisane.

(27) Brinjal Foogath, Rasam, plain puris, Quick Relishes.

(28) Burgers in Thick Barbecue Sauce, Hot Herb Slaw, chilled soft drinks.

(29) Hawaiian Rice Pineapple, Cold Breaded Gluten, Plum Sauce, China tea.

(30) Sliced Klops, Mushroom and Potato Zharkoye, sauerkraut, fresh plums.

(31) Huguenot Soup, Little Cauliflower Fritters, Chicory Plum Salad, Tapioca Grape Jell.

(32) Bauernspeise, Stuffed Mangoes, Chimpanzees' Delight, rose-hip tisane.

(33) Swallows' Nests, Chilled Stuffed Tomatoes, bryndza cheese, fresh fruit.

(34) Moroccan Potatoes, Salata Mechouia, fresh peach Fruit Tarts.

(35) Antipasto, Mushroom-Walnut Pancakes, Maize Galettes, coffee.

(36) Greens and Egg-Froth Soup, Soft-Fried Noodles, Soy-Cooked Watercress, Cold Breaded Gluten, Plum Sauce, very dry sherry.

(37) Vegetable Chop Suey, Dry-Cooked Rice, Mushroom Fried Almonds, Fried-Stirred Celery, fresh plums.

(38) Mushroom Watercress Soup, Dry-Cooked Rice, Breaded

Gluten Sweet and Sour, Fried-Stirred Cabbage, jasmine tea.

(39) White Mushroom and Ginger Soup, Soft-Fried Noodles, Fried-Stirred Bean Sprouts, Fried-Stirred Mushrooms, Egg Rolls, Oolong tea.

(40) Burgers, Sweet Potato Mash, Flavoury Radishes, Honey and Nut Pizzas.

(41) Pickled baby aubergines, Fava, white bread chunks, Honeyed Wine Vegetables, yoghourt with fruit conserve.

(42) At-Once-Soup, Fried Rice, Breaded Gluten Pineapple, Red-Cooked Mushroom, Green Simmer, tea.

(43) Potato Fruit Cakes, Avocado Vegetable Salad, Little Clotted Cream Gateaux.

(44) Felaffel with Felaffel Hot Sauce, Summer Salad, dried pears and nuts.

(45) Finocchio del Padrone, Salade Benvenuto, Golden Berry Custard.

(46) Délice de Champignons, Kasha and Baby Marrows, fresh fruit.

(47) Aubergine Fritters with lemon wedges, Salade Niçoise, French bread, wine.

(48) Woodland Casserole, tomatoes and cucumbers in wine vinegar, strawberries and sour cream.

(49) Stuffed Potato Bake, Dill-Pickled Cucumbers, Sweet Semolina Halwa.

(50) Spiced Gluten Kebab, Green Peppers and Potatoes, bowl of fresh fruit.

SNACKS

(1) Gaspacho, chilled wine.

(2) Olives and Cheese, crusty bread.

(3) Hermit's Bread, stout.

(4) Grilled Corn on the Cob with plenty of butter, salt and pepper.

(5) Antipasto with *grissini*, lemon tea.

(6) Mushroom Pâté on thin crisp biscuits, dry sherry.

(7) Samosas, and yoghourt flavoured with chopped chilli peppers.

(8) Goldy Green Spread on buttered rye bread, green and black olives.

(9) Grilled Olive Bread, rich creamy coffee.

(10) Spicy Chick Pea Puffs, cocktails.

(11)   Toasted buttered bagels spread with Chopped Herring without Herring, coffee.
(12)   "Taramasalata" on buttered toast, lemon tea.
(13)   Garlic Bread, young red wine.
(14)   Foil-Baked Potatoes, Dill-Pickled Cucumbers, beer.
(15)   Egg Rolls, Plum Sauce, jasmine tea.
(16)   Pain Perdu Québecois, milky coffee.
(17)   Avocado Chilli Dip, toast fingers.
(18)   Potato Bonda, chutneys.
(19)   Boiled new potatoes with Green Aioli, wine.
(20)   Curried Gluten, Fulouries, soft drinks.

Vitamins, Protein and Minerals

We draw from our food the nutritive material necessary for growth, stamina and energy. A good supply of vitamins, minerals and protein protects, maintains and repairs the body tissues.

From the widely differing varieties of fruits, vegetables, nuts and cereals used in this book, a short list has been compiled to give an indication of the nutritive values of natural foods.

VITAMINS

Vitamins are organic substances essential for life and health which the body is unable to form for itself. Found in natural, unrefined foods.

VITAMIN A and CAROTENE   Protect the lining of the respiratory tract, throat and bronchial tubes; also for healthy functioning of eyes. (Carotene is a pigment which when absorbed into the body may be converted into Vitamin A. The greener the vegetable, the greater the amount of carotene it contains.)

Some food containing Vitamin A or Carotene

apricots (dried); avocados; beans (green); cabbage; carrots; celery (green); cheese; coriander (green); corn-on-the-cob; egg yolk; lettuce; milk; parsley; peppers (sweet green); peas (green); prunes; mint (raw); mustard and cress; spinach; turnip tops; watercress.

VITAMIN B COMPLEX   The most comprehensive in its functions: aids appetite, growth, revitalizes. Comprises a number of substances often, but not always, found together in the same foods. The main members of the group are *Thiamine, Riboflavin* and *Nicotinic Acid.*

Some foods containing Vitamin B Complex

ales; asparagus; beans; bean sprouts (fresh); bread (wholemeal); brussels sprouts; buttermilk; cereals (whole); gluten (wheat); lentils (dals); maize meal; millet; peanuts; potatoes; semolina; sesame seeds; soya beans; walnuts; wheat germ; yeast; yoghourt.

VITAMIN C Aids resistance to infections, promotes healthy healing of wounds and fractures. Cannot be stored by the body and must be renewed daily. Easily destroyed in cooking, so *raw* fruits and vegetables should form part of the daily diet.

Some foods containing Vitamin C
avocados; bean sprouts (fresh); blackcurrants; brussels sprouts (raw); cabbage; cauliflower; coriander (green); cucumber; grapefruit; horseradish; lemons; limes; oranges; parsley (raw); peppers (sweet green and red); raspberries; spinach; strawberries; tangerines; tomatoes.

VITAMIN D Essential for aiding teeth and bones to retain calcium and phosphorus. Normalises some glandular functions. Particularly important for expectant mothers and infants.

Some foods containing Vitamin D
butter; cheese; eggs; margarine fortified with Vitamin D; milk.

VITAMIN E There is evidence (not yet conclusive) that Vitamin E plays a part in influencing fertility in human beings.

Some foods containing Vitamin E
lettuce; milk; peas; watercress; wheat germ.

VITAMIN K Essential for normal clotting of blood.

Some foods containing Vitamin K
cabbage (Savoy); peas (green); spinach; watercress.

PROTEIN

Protein is an essential constituent of plant and animal cells. There is no living matter without protein, which is necessary for growth, repair of body tissues, and stamina.

Some foods containing protein
almonds; batavia; brussels sprouts; butter beans; cereals (whole); cheese; eggs; gluten (wheat); lentils (dals); milk; oatmeal; peanuts; potatoes (old); walnuts; wheat germ; yeast.

COMPARATIVE PROTEIN VALUES

1 oz. beef sirloin   = 1 oz. almonds
(or fried sole, cod, plaice)   or $\frac{1}{2}$ cup lentils
     ,, $\frac{3}{4}$ oz. peanuts
     ,, 1 oz. gouda cheese
     ,, 1 oz. cottage cheese

„ $\frac{3}{4}$ cup skimmed milk
„ $1\frac{1}{2}$ oz. welsh rarebit

1 oz. beef stew   = $\frac{1}{2}$ egg
or $\frac{1}{2}$ oz. almonds
„ $\frac{1}{2}$ cup whole milk
„ 1 oz. dried apricots and $\frac{1}{2}$ oz. walnuts
„ 1 oz. oatmeal
„ $1\frac{1}{4}$ oz. brown bread
„ 2 oz. spinach

MINERALS

Minerals are necessary constituents of bones, teeth and body cells. Some maintain the normal alkaline-acid balance of the blood, others regulate the digestive processes.

CALCIUM   Maintenance of strong bones and teeth.

Some foods containing calcium
almonds; broccoli; cabbage (outer leaves); cheese; milk; parsley; seaweed; spinach; spring onions; watercress.

PHOSPHORUS   Plays an essential part in the life of all body cells. Present in significant amounts in natural foods.

IRON   Anti-anaemia factor. Necessary for transport of oxygen to the tissues.

Some foods containing iron
aubergines; beans (french); celeriac; egg yolk; endive; leeks; lentils (dals); médoc; mustard and cress; parsley (raw); prunes; raspberries; watercress; yeast.

POTASSIUM   Gives the body fluids the stability essential to life. Present in significant amounts in natural foods.

IODINE   Necessary for normal functioning of thyroid gland.

Some foods containing iodine
bananas; cheese; cherries; milk.

*   *   *

Most of the material in this section is based on data derived from *The Composition of Foods* by R. A. McCance, CBE, MD, PH.D, FRCP, FRS, and E. M. Widdowson, D.SC (Medical

Research Council Special Report Series, 1960) and from the *Manual of Nutrition* (published for the Ministry of Agriculture, 1961), both issued by Her Majesty's Stationery Office.

We are especially indebted to Frank Wokes, PH.D, B.SC, FRIC, FPS, who read over the section and made many valuable suggestions.

Index